EXPLORING ESSEX BY WHEEL

JOHN COULSON

IAN HENRY PUBLICATIONS

ISBN 0 86025 471 2

Printed by
Redwood Books, Ltd.
Kennet House, Kennet Way, Trowbridge, Wiltshire BA14 8RN
for
Ian Henry Publications, Ltd.
20 Park Drive, Romford, Essex, RM1 4LH

PREFACE

A friend of mine, a Midlander, once remarked to me in some astonishment that he had not realised Essex was so hilly, having for the first time heaved a tandem over the tail-end of the Chiltern range which straggles across into the far north-western corner of the county. He confided that he had hitherto regarded Essex as little more than ugly car factories sitting on dreary marshland and was agreeably surprised to find that closer acquaintance brought an entirely different view.

His ingrained misconception was typical of that of many others whose knowledge of the county is little more than the arterial road and rail routes from London to the Essex and East Anglian coast which offer small clue to the delights to be found even a short distance on either side. Nobody would pretend that Essex is spectacular, except in respect of certain architectural gems: her charms are of a far more subtle kind, a gentle harmony of line and colour to be savoured in unhurried exploration. She casts a spell on those who seek her out in this way, a magic composed of many ingredients, from the summer sunlight shimmering across the wide spaces of the Rodings to the aura of history surrounding many old villages and towns, to a windy day in late autumn in Epping Forest, the ground ablaze with a myriad fallen leaves.

Perhaps much of the appeal of the Essex countryside lies in its abiding feeling of remoteness despite its proximity to London and the efforts of the motorway builders to savage its fair face. Certainly, for the cyclist, it is an almost perfect area. Few other counties of Britain are blessed with such a network of lanes and byroads which, even today, carry remarkably little motor traffic by comparison with the vehicle density of the 'A' class highways.

My own introduction to the Essex byways was idyllic. As a young teenager at the end of the Second World War I was given a bicycle which was to open up my horizons beyond Epping

1

Forest, already thoroughly explored on foot. There was no traffic; petrol was stringently rationed, the developers and town planners had yet to extend their ravages much more than ten miles from the centre of London, the countryside was still much as I imagined it from reading Victorian and Edwardian school stories and I embarked on a love affair with cycling the highways and byways of Essex that has lasted a lifetime.

Although the proliferation of the motor car has robbed Essex of a little of that erstwhile utter timelessness, and some of its choicest landscape has succumbed to the relentless march of bricks and mortar and concrete, much of the essential Essex still awaits our searching wheels.

In the following pages I have described fifteen routes, seeking out some of the best of Essex, any of which can be accomplished by a reasonably experienced cyclist within a day. Some need occupy only a morning or afternoon; some can be linked to form a longer route if desired and short cuts and alternatives are indicated where they might be useful. Most of the routes involve some mileage in narrow lanes with restricted visibility ahead and care needs to be exercised, particularly if riding in a group.

Rail connections are not what they were, but are mentioned as appropriate, with the proviso that an intending user is advised to check availability beforehand. In line with the modern trend for cyclists to motor out into the countryside to start a ride I have indicated places where, in my experience, cars may be left safely for a few hours.

I emphasise that this is no sort of a cycle touring manual. Although I have not aimed specifically at the legion of club riders who have been my companions most of my life, I have assumed that my readers can read a map and have already acquired some interest and expertise in cycling. All my own cycling in Britain has done with reference to some of the best maps in the world, Ordnance Survey and Bartholomew's, and the relevant sheet numbers appear in the heading of each route. However, I have to deliver a caveat inasmuch as the latest Bartholomew's series is not up to the standard of the old, well-loved Half Inch maps and even those, like Homer, nodded occasionally.

None of the rides is hard in the sense that a tour of Devon and Cornwall is hard, but then, as all experienced cyclists know, any ride anywhere is as hard or easy as one cares to make it. Any of my routes could be dealt with happily on a machine with a single gear of around 65" as long as one is prepared to press harder on the pedals from time to time or walk the occasional hill as the mood indicates. Here and there we use a bridle-path or farm track but there is nothing which cannot be tackled with a light touring machine, still the pleasantest way of covering the ground despite the advent of the All Terrain Bicycle.

Although the rides described carry an indication of severity and mileage (I still adhere to miles rather than kilometres as all signposts are still in miles - and I prefer English miles anyway!) they are not intended as training routes for competitive riders, although they could well serve as such, but rather for touring cyclists who are interested in what is about them. Thus I have pointed out some of the abundant historical, literary and artistic associations as appropriate and indulged in the occasional anecdote so that my cycling readers might feel that we are in company on the road or perhaps planning our jaunts together from a winter armchair. It is my hope that this will be found not merely a cycling guidebook but more an insight into a quiet, almost secretive county too often unjustly maligned in the popular media. It is impossible in the space available to include every item of interest in Essex, but I hope the routes described will serve to whet the reader's appetite and prove an inspiration to go out and explore and enjoy my native county awheel as I have done for over half a century.

3

All Saints, High Laver. Within the railings is the tomb of John Locke

CHAPTER I

Romford - Navestock - Moreton - Matching - Theydon Mount - Romford
44 miles with diversions. First and last sections hilly.
OS Landranger sheets 167 & 177. Bartholomew's Leisure Map Essex

The ride assumes a start in or around Romford. Once a pleasant country market town Romford is now virtually an outer suburb of London and suffered grievously in the widespread architectural vandalism perpetrated in the sixties. However, it has two railway stations convenient for our purpose, Romford and Gidea Park, and there are numerous quiet streets in the Gidea Park area where a car may be left without inconvenience to local residents. The multi-storey car parks in central Romford are not recommended because of possible vandalism.

There is nothing truly of interest to us as cyclists until we have cleared the traffic and picked up the B175 northward out of town and are climbing Orange Tree Hill. On the right among the trees as we climb is Bower House, built in 1729 on the site of the Royal Palace of Havering and allegedly haunted. It is now owned by the Ford Motor Company and doubtless the sceptical Henry Ford would have classed hauntings in with his view of the rest of history as 'bunk'.

We are here tackling one of the stiffest climbs on the route but the reward is the view southward from the top where we are in Havering-atte-Bower village, one of the higher points in Essex. The panorama extends across the slopes of Bedfords Park, once a private estate and now a popular public open space, to the Thames and beyond to the North Downs. On the green stand the stocks, not the centuries old originals but a cosmetic replacement, and the church facing us across the green is popular with local artists and for fashionable weddings. Eastward from the green along Broxhill Road a striking water tower, erected in 1934 and a landmark for many miles, stands almost opposite the entrance to Bedfords Park. The park is worth a diversion, although the mansion is long demolished, and is a useful place to leave a car, bearing in mind that the park closes at sunset.

Havering village has given its name to the London Borough which contains it and has ancient royal connections, legend telling us that Havering derives from a medieval king offering his ring to a beggar - "have a ring". Charming though this may be I fancy the real derivation is rather more mundane and it is merely Anglo-Saxon for "the Folks who live on the Hill".

Returning to our route we skirt the green to drop down North Road past pleasant bungalows till, swinging left and starting to climb gently we come to Tysea Hill on the right, into which we turn. A gentle drop and a short, sharp climb bring us to a junction with a deconsecrated chapel on the corner and we ignore the turning on the right to continue straight on into Murthering Lane. This narrow highway, in particular, needs our attention to pot-holes, farm dogs and other livestock wandering in the roadway. The name is a dialect corruption of murdering and commemorates a notorious murder in 1927 when PC Gutteridge, the local policeman, was shot dead while trying to arrest two car thieves. The singular feature of the crime was that the murderers shot out the unfortunate officer's eyes in the superstitious belief that the retinas retained the image of the killers after death. Both criminals were subsequently arrested, tried and hanged.

We are now in true rural Essex, little changed since I first rode these lanes fifty years ago, high hedges and copses on either side, and it is a rude shock to find ourselves suddenly crossing high above the howling M25 motorway where the view expands on our left across the Roding valley to the hills through which we shall soon be making our way.

Fortunately, we soon leave the motorway racket behind and in a mile or so reach the open space of Navestock Heath, the

Plough Inn beckoning in its far corner if we are already thirsty. At the far side of the heath we turn left at the T-junction to drop down tree-lined Church Road to make another left turn at the bottom. In a short distance we can make a diversion to the right to see Navestock church with magnificent 13th Century woodwork supporting its belfry and beside it the half-timbered exterior of Navestock Hall. It is a sobering thought that this idyllic setting was recently under threat from the proposed M12 motorway, now mercifully shelved. The church car park, incidentally, can be used to leave a car if necessary, assuming no church functions are in progress.

Continuing westwards now we climb a little before dropping down to Shonks Mill bridge over the River Roding, which is liable to flood here after heavy rain and the road beyond is occasionally impassable. However, this is rare and we can usually press on to climb gently up to the A113, where we turn right, giving attention to fast-moving traffic, and then in some 200 yards, left into the peace of narrow Berwick Lane, almost opposite the Elizabethan-style chimneys of Lawns farmhouse.

Berwick Lane climbs steadily for almost two miles through woodland and high banks, past the occasional cottage and farm-house, till we swing right on the level with Knightsland Wood on the left and a view eastward over the Roding valley on the right. Early summer in these lanes is delightful, the heady aroma of the broad bean blossom displacing the acrid small of the now-fading rape fields, their blaze of yellow blossom giving way to the blue-green sheen of an Essex summer.

We drop down a winding descent past a golf course to turn left at the bottom and start immediately on the stiff climb up to Toot Hill. The village, not overly attractive, stands on a commanding height, and the name almost certainly derives from the Celtic word for a lookout point. We bear right at the triangular green and a welcome downhill spin brings us to Greensted Green. Our route turns left here but a diversion of about a mile and a half to the right brings us to Greensted church, widely famed for its walls of split oak which have survived over a thousand years since they were hewn by their Saxon builders. The church car park makes another convenient place to leave a vehicle.

Retracing to Greensted Green we continue over the railway bridge at Blake Hall station, which is now closed although the building still exists as a private house. Indeed, the entire single track from Epping to Ongar, until recently part of the London Transport system, has now closed, although there is a preservation movement afoot to re-establish steam trains, last run here in 1957.

We drop swiftly downhill to cross the A414 in another mile - beware fast-moving traffic here - before climbing up to Bobbingworth, pronounced Bovinger by all true Essex folk, to turn right near the top. Past the church we turn sharp left, leaving Blake Hall itself on the right; the gardens are sometimes open to the public on summer weekends. Ignoring a byway turning off a right hand bend we turn left again in less than a mile for the descent into Moreton.

This village has an attractive approach over Cripsey Brook and there are two pubs, the White Hart and the Moreton Massey, formerly the Nag's Head, both of which cater adequately for cycling appetites. The White Hart in the early years of this century was the luncheon venue for the famous Woodford Meet, when hundreds of riders congregated once a year at Woodford Green to ride in all manner of fancy dress via Epping to Moreton.

We turn left around the White Hart to move northward again. C. V. Smith's *A Cockney Boy in Essex* is a mine of information on Moreton as it was early in the century and he tells us that Brook Lodge, on our left in about half a mile, was once also a pub, the Pig and Whistle. Along a turning on the right once stood Moreton windmill, pulled down, alas, some time in the fifties.

Following our road through numerous twists and turns we

come to High Laver church on the north east corner of a cross roads. Against the south wall of the church is a monument, placed by the American and British Commonwealth Association of the United States, to the writer and philosopher John Locke, who is buried here and whose beliefs had a profound influence on the writing of the American constitution.

Continuing ahead on an easy road we come at length to our approximate halfway point at Matching Green. A short distance to the right as the green opens out is the Chequers Inn, where cyclists are always welcome and an ideal place to lunch and loiter, with maybe a game of cricket in progress on the attractive green. In the house next door to the Chequers the painter Augustus John lived for a number of years and in a cottage on the north side of the green once lived a character famous for the grotesque concrete figures of his own making which adorned his front garden, and for his home-made dentures of the same material!

From to the green we can turn north along the Hatfield Heath road till we come to a lane on the left signed Matching Church and marked as a dead end. This will take us down and around a beautiful lake, teeming with bird life, and then sharply up to Matching church. Beside the church, facing a small green, is the Feast House, built around 1480 for village wedding celebrations and other functions. A group of us were once lucky enough to be given an impromptu conducted tour of the interior by the vicar who congratulated us on our mode of transport, enthused about his parish and assured us this was certainly the oldest, and possibly the only, surviving building of this type in the country. On the green is an oak tree planted in 1887 in honour of Queen Victoria's Golden Jubilee. We may note with some surprise the American spelling 'honor' on the plaque.

Beyond the green the road becomes a private bridle-path, with humps to deter use by motorists, but as cyclists we are permitted to use it and by making two left turns once back on public road we come to the hamlet of Matching Tye. We turn right and then left beyond the houses to Carters Green and by making three more left turns we let these delightful lanes bring us gently back to High Laver church. Retracing our outward route for half a mile towards Moreton we turn right again to undulate gently as far as Weald Lodge where two left turns take us through pleasant Ashlyns Lane almost to the A414 again. However, we can avoid any mileage on this by a sharp left back towards Moreton and then a right, and right again to retrace our outward route as far as Toot Hill.

Here we bear right at the green to tackle a difficult switchback mile and a half before the last climb up to Colliers Hatch brings us out on a mile of Roman road, straight and fairly level. We are high here, rolling landscape stretches away to the left and as we dip sharply down and right at the end of the straight a clear day will show us the tall buildings in the centre of London etching the skyline like a row of broken teeth. In a few yards we turn left to dip even more sharply down through Mount End. This is a fast descent and needs care, particularly in view of the distracting panorama opening out across to the Epping Forest ridge. At the bottom our Roman road continues ahead as a bridleway but we turn sharp left up the steepest climb of the day, Theydon Mount, included on the route of more than one testing race. Once over the top the road undulates past the grounds of Hill Hall, now demolished but once a women's prison, and on the skyline beyond the Roding we can see the water tower at Havering-atte-Bower betokening the approaching end of our ride.

However, some of the hardest miles in Essex now await us. The run down off Theydon Mount takes us over the thundering M25 to a left turn at a T-junction and eventually alongside the motorway to the A113 where a right turn brings us to the roundabout at Passingford Bridge. In my youth there was a green triangle where the traffic now gyrates and the bridge was a narrow, brick, three-arched affair with a placid lily pool beneath, among trees. All was swept away in the sixties when the authorities did not see fit to bypass it and thus preserve a fragment of a more leisurely age, as has been done elsewhere.

The B175 will give us three stiff climbs before we reach journey's end but fortunately there are several hostelries to sustain us on the way if necessary and it is worth stopping half-way down the first long descent to see the tablet recently placed on the left to the memory of the PC Gutteridge mentioned earlier and to note that the dog-leg of old road, now bypassed, also bears his name.

A glance at the map will show that there are many places where this route may be shortened if desired: as described it is a respectable day's ride, but railway connections at Harlow or Epping, for instance, would convert it readily into a one-way route if preferred.

Winter sunshine on a frozen Matching pond

CHAPTER 2

Ingatestone - Writtle - Roxwell - Fyfield - Willingale - Blackmore
- Ingatestone.
35 miles with diversions. Gently undulating with a few moderate
climbs.
OS Landranger sheet 167. Bartholomew's Leisure Map Essex.

Ingatestone is a long-established village on the old Roman road
from London to Colchester and despite having expanded
considerably over the last forty years into a small dormitory
town it still retains some of its rural appeal by virtue of now
being bypassed by the A12 trunk road. Moreover it has a railway
station and swift access to country roads on either side. For the
car-borne, parking may be a little difficult on weekdays due to
commuter pressures, but at weekends space can usually be found
in the free car park towards the eastern end of the High Street,
formerly the main road to Chelmsford, Colchester and the coast.
Some empirical research will find other spots although it is
important to pay attention to part-time parking restrictions.
There is another alternative which I shall mention shortly.

Our ride starts effectively from the cramped crossroads in
the middle of the village near the church. We take Fryerning Lane
north-westwards - the entrance is narrow and it is easy to miss
- to climb steadily away from the High Street and in a few
hundred yards cross the roaring A12. Almost immediately we are
in rural surroundings and the road leads in half a mile to the
Woolpack Inn with Fryerning church away to the left. We turn
right here and, ignoring lanes to right and left, continue ahead on
a well-surfaced road past large tree-shrouded houses which make
Mill Green seem more typical of Surrey than of Essex. Passing the
Cricketers Inn on our right we come to the green itself where
there is a convenient car parking area. The green is enclosed by
trees and beyond it we plunge into deep, delightful woodland,

chest-high with bracken in late summer. In the middle of the wood we pass another pub, the Viper, on our left. At the junction beyond it we dip sharply away to our left, taking care on the long, swinging bends to emerge from the wood and undulate a mile and a half past open fields to a T-junction. We turn right here with care as the right-hand approach is a little blind, and tackle the steady rise up to Loves Green. The Ordnance Survey indicates moats on the left here, but they are on private property and I have never seen them.

We drop gently down to bear right by Loves Green church and climb the rise to Edney Common - the villages appear together on the road sign. Two hundred yards beyond the Green Man pub here we can make a diversion along a gritty but rideable lane on the right which will bring us in under a mile to Writtle Park, the seat of Lord Petre, who owns much of the land hereabouts. The house is private but in a field opposite stands a prominent circular building which, so I am informed by a local inhabitant, was a dovecote. However, there is no apparent means of ingress or egress for the birds and from the presence of a closely slatted window and a hefty door I am inclined to the view that it could equally well have been the village lock-up.

Returning to our route we turn eastward again for an easy downhill two miles to Great Oxney Green. We are now easing out into the wide, rolling cornlands of central Essex and, when I was reconnoitring the route prior to setting down these words, the land was glowing gold with ripening harvest. Approaching Oxney Green our pleasant spin is interrupted by the new Writtle bypass, part of the busy A414, and we must negotiate a roundabout with care to take the second exit which will bring us shortly to another roundabout where we swing right into Great Oxney Green village. In about two hundred yards we turn left at a small crossroads and reach the Victoria Inn in another two hundred yards.

Turning left we leave the little cluster of houses behind and follow a lane which dips and winds pleasantly and leaving the quaintly named Cow Watering Lane on the right we press on to Newney Green where the Duck Inn will sustain us if need be. A short distance beyond the Duck we turn right into a narrow lane, hedged at first, then opening out to an expanse of fields, which drops us gently down to another junction where a left turn and a gentle climb bring us to Roxwell. There was once a tea place here in a cottage which one entered through the back garden, but this is long gone and, even though the Chequers Inn next to the church opens its doors all day, Roxwell conveys the air of a place where nothing ever happens, save at school times when there is a flurry of young mothers dropping off or collecting their off-spring. At the western end of the village we swing right and left over Roxwell Brook, ignoring a turning on the right, and commence a climb which is gentle but lengthy, being the best part of three miles long. With an east wind the gradient is barely noticeable but a brisk westerly can make it something of a chore. However, the scenery is pleasant and hiding away somewhere to our left is Skreens Park, a centre for the Scouting and Guiding movement. 'Rough-stuffing' some field paths here many years ago one of our party was chased across a large meadow by a herd of exceedingly frolicsome cows while the rest of us withdrew hastily behind the gate. Fortunately, as an agile young racing man, he was able to outpace the cows, as we later discovered.

When we reach the former church, still recognizable by its tiny belfry, at the oddly-named Shellow Bowells we have topped the climb. The graveyard still exists, though over-grown, and some cycling wag might suggest that many of us have 'died' on the climb in westerly gales, but the church has been a private residence for some fifteen years.

Half a mile further on, on the right, we come to a tree-lined avenue leading to Torrells Hall, a large farm. This is a bridleway although not at present signposted as such and we trundle along here to turn sharp right actually in the farmyard at the end. A metalled lane leads on and eventually left and following this brings us to Berners Roding. This is now virtually a dead village, most of the few cottages still standing are uninhabited and nothing but the foundations of several others remain. The tiny church building still stands, forlornly empty and unused and so overgrown as to be invisible from the road. It can be reached by those who do not mind a rash of nettle stings along a footpath running north along the west side of Berners Hall farm. One grave is still tended, that of one of the Meads family, of whom more shortly.

There are many deer in the countryside hereabouts, they are often seen on the fields in winter and in fact, a companion and I were nearly bowled over by a herd of about a dozen a few winters ago.

In another half-mile we reach a T-junction and a half-mile diversion to the right will bring us to Waples Mill, sometimes spelt Whaypules Mill. This was formerly owned by Isaac Meads, a member of the family just mentioned, who was born in 1859 and came to own several mills in Essex. Towards the end of his life he wrote his autobiography, *The Life Story of an Essex Lad*, containing a wealth of information on this part of Essex. There were once two mills at Waples, water and wind. Part of the water mill still stands on the left, between the road and the smooth-flowing River Roding, but the windmill which stood on the higher ground opposite was burnt down in 1910 and no trace of it can now be seen.

Retracing, we continue straight on to bear right, ignoring a byway and then a road on the left to cross the Roding and arrive in a few hundred yards at Birds Green. Opposite a turning on the left is a house called Two Swans, formerly a cosy little pub of that name often crammed to bursting point with convivial cyclists. If we continue to bear right here we can climb the hill for half a mile to Hornets Farm on the left, where lived Isaac Meads during the latter part of his life and where there is a private family cemetery, neglected and over-grown, on the corner the drive. Isaac Meads' wife is certainly buried here and in all probability the author himself, although an essential part of the inscription on the tombstone is regrettably obscured by a later addition.

Two churches in one churchyard - Willingdale Doe and Willingale Spain

Returning to Birds Green we take the road opposite Two Swans and after a gentle climb and an equally gentle descent find ourselves meeting the B184. A left turn here takes us shortly into Fyfield where, if lunch is indicated, there are two pubs, the Black Bull and, even better, the Queen's Head, where the landlord will always bandy cheerful words with cyclists and recommend them to try various outlandish ales from all corners of Britain. On warm days we can sit in the garden here with the Roding sliding past at our feet.

Suitably refreshed, we turn along the road beside the Queen's Head towards Willingale, crossing the Roding again to start a lengthy climb by the church. Three miles of zig-zagging undulations will bring us with a last stiff climb to Willingale, but before we reach it we shall notice dilapidated military type buildings here and there to the right of the road. These are the remains of Willingale airfield, a relic of World War II, used for cycle racing in the early fifties and mooted in the late seventies as a possible third London airport, perhaps as a diversionary measure from the already-planned extension of Stansted, further north. However, a strong protest movement won the day, with the support of many cyclists incidentally, and Willingale retains its rural somnolence to the point where the Maltsters' Arms rarely sees a midday customer during the week apart from occasional passing cyclists. Opposite the Maltsters' Arms the main street drops gently down to the unique feature of the village, two churches in one churchyard, a reminder that Willingale was formerly two parishes, Willingale Doe and Willingale Spain, the former parish boundary running between them and now marked by the Essex Way long-distance footpath.

The little shingle-spired church of Willingale Spain is no longer used and the larger, towered church of Willingale Doe now serves both parishes as well as the once separate parish of Shellow. Opposite the churches is Bell House, the Bell Inn until a few years ago, now, alas, gone the way of so many others in the modern climate of maximum profit.

From the Maltsters' Arms we continue eastward, forking right to pedal past Spains Hall and we might well wonder whether airport planners and their like ever know or care what havoc they proposed to create in an area such as this. Nevertheless it is worth reflecting that the wide landscape on which we are feasting our eyes is almost entirely man-made here in Essex, a harmonious adaptation of the forces of nature in the great industry of agriculture.

After dropping down to a junction where we turn sharp right we start a steady three-mile climb around numerous bends up to the heights of Norton Heath where graceful woods hide the remains of brickworks diggings, probably used in the construction of Norton Manor opposite whose chimneys are worth more than a second glance.

There is a café here on the old main road, now by-passed, well patronized by lorry drivers, indicating a cheap, basic and satisfying menu, which also makes it popular with cyclists.

Norton Heath is now bypassed by the A414 and if we turn westwards from the cafe we shall meet the main road in about two hundred yards and, turning right with due attention to fast-moving traffic, in a similar distance we fork left at a garage into Rookery Road. A gentle descent and a gentle climb bring us to Nine Ashes where, after passing King Street on our right, we reach Nine Ashes Road on our left in about a mile. Our route turns left here but a diversion of another mile straight ahead through the expensive detached properties of Nine Ashes brings us to Paslow Wood Common where the Black Horse pub has long been a popular meeting place for Essex cyclists. It carries a large Cyclists' Touring Club sign on its front wall, not one of the cast iron originals from the pre-1914 era but a convincing hand-made imitation fashioned, with CTC permission, by two local cycling artists.

Retracing to our original route we drop down the long descent to Blackmore with, reputedly, the largest field in Essex on our right and the village church thrusting up out of the trees

Norton Manor, Norton Heath

Blackmore Pond

in the valley bottom. Just before we reach the village we pass Red Rose Lane on our left. This is known locally as the Plague Road and was made, so the story goes, in the time of the Black Death to enable travellers to bypass the village and thus avoid bringing the plague to it. Blackmore is now very much a commuter village but nonetheless still retains an attractive character and a strong community spirit. Our long run down from Nine Ashes has brought us to Horsefayre Green in the centre of the village where there are two pubs, the Prince Albert and the Leather Bottle, and on the north side of the green an antique shop which also serves teas.

There is a third pub, the Bull, tucked away in a street of old houses leading to the church on the south side of the village, half-timbered with a jettied upper storey, somewhat expensive and none the better for that. The church is noteworthy as a large example of the typical Essex religious house, shingled spire and weatherboarded belfry rising pagoda-like above half-timbered base, and particularly for the four huge hewn oak uprights rising from ground level to support the belfry and spire. These 15th century constructions conceal a Norman doorway and window at the west end of the nave. The churchyard has an area left deliberately in a wild state to attract butterflies and other insects.

Behind the church lie the remains of Jericho Priory. This was destroyed by order of Henry VIII, although apparently he was not averse to using the original house, now replaced with a more modern structure, as a hideaway when matters of state became too pressing! Hence the expression "Go to Jericho".

Of the original priory buildings, only part of the outer wall and moat now remain for us to inspect. Returning to Horsefayre Green we turn right alongside the green proper. We may notice a white line painted across the road here, a relic of several recent years when Blackmore imitated the Continental example by running 'round-the-houses' cycle racing in conjunction with the village fête. Crossing between the two ponds at the bottom end of the green we turn right and after swinging left in about a mile find ourselves tackling a long climb up through woodlands, a sign that we are approaching the environs of Ingatestone once more. Making sure that we take the next on the left beyond the trees of Fryerning Wood our road will take us straight ahead to the sharp climb up to Fryerning church and thence with a right turn down into Ingatestone and the end of the ride.

The dovecote - or is it a lock-up? - by Writtle Park

CHAPTER 3

Sawbridgeworth - Stort Navigation - Hatfield Forest - Hatfield Heath - Sawbridgeworth.
17 miles. Mainly easy riding with some undulations.
OS Landranger sheet 167. Bartholomew's Leisure Map Essex.

This short ride starts with a little cheating because, in fact, it starts just in Hertfordshire where that county pokes a finger into Essex across the River Stort, which for much of its course forms the Essex/Hertford boundary. The incursion was presumably to include the estates of Great and Little Hyde Halls within Hertfordshire, perhaps for parliamentary reasons.

However, of more concern to us is that Sawbridgeworth railway station is conveniently placed for the start of our ride and there is also car parking opposite the station, cheap on weekdays and free at weekends.

Leaving the station and heading west towards the town we come in a couple of hundred yards to an arm of the old River Stort and, just beyond it, the delightful Stort Navigation, where lies our immediate objective, the towpath running northwards along its eastern bank. The towpath is easily ridden on any sort of machine although naturally a certain amount of care is needed, particularly around deep water at locks and weirs. For those who have no fancy for towpath riding and prefer to stick to metalled roads there is an alternative which I shall mention at the end of the chapter.

The navigation dates back well over 200 years and was a logical extension of the canalization of the River Lea (or Lee), parts of which have been navigable since Roman times. Although there was doubtless some traffic to the maltings at Sawbridgeworth, just at our backs, and also to those at Bishops Stortford, five miles upstream, commercial traffic on the Stort Navigation has never been of great significance owing to the

The Stort Navigation from the bridge at Spellbrook Lane

The Shell House in Hatfield Forest

proposed canal from Bishop's Stortford to Cambridge failing to materialise. The waterway is now given over almost entirely to pleasure boating and as we reach Sawbridgeworth lock in a little over a quarter of a mile we could well indulge in a few minutes' 'gongoozling' as a cruiser is locked through by its crew.

Just beyond this lock is the only real obstacle we shall encounter. This is a kissing-gate, erected,one suspects, to discourage the likes of us from sullying the preserves of the Sawbridgeworth Angling Society. However, a bicycle can be wriggled through by standing it on its rear wheel or, with companions, lifted over. We pass under the London-Cambridge railway line and in a few hundred yards are in Essex, where we should rightly be. There are gates to negotiate, placed to prevent cattle straying, but neither they nor the cattle themselves should present us with any problem. At Tednambury lock we are in idyllic seclusion; a backwater provides moorings for cruisers and a glance at the map shows that the oxbow has put us briefly back in Hertfordshire till we cross the bridge beyond the lock. A further half-mile of bird-haunted waterside meadow brings us to hard road again, just short of Spellbrook lock and about two and a half miles from Sawbridgeworth.

We turn right here and uphill around the edge of the large ancient earthwork of Wallbury Camp. This is on private land and cannot be inspected although in truth there is little to see apart from the high surrounding bank. Beyond Wallbury we pass some pleasant houses to emerge on the A1060 at George Green, so called after a pub of that name. Here we turn right for half a mile until we reach Little Hallingbury church nestling among trees where we turn left. In a short distance our road swings right and almost immediately we find Goose Lane on our left. Turning into this our route takes us rising gently past modern housing development on our right to cross the M11 motorway before levelling out across open fields.

Rattling across a cattlegrid we turn sharp left and find Woodside Green opening out unexpectedly before us. This is

National Trust property, a long green forming part of the Forest Way long distance footpath. Cottages cluster along the western side and on the roadside by Thimble Cottage there is a tiny village lock-up hardly bigger than a telephone kiosk. Local farmers have the right to graze their cattle on the green and as we follow the road snaking round its edge we may notice how the undersides of some of the trees have been browsed level by the animals. At length we reach a T-junction and turn right along the northern edge of the green, crossing another cattle grid as we leave it, a fine avenue of horse chestnut, oak and ash trees by Lodge Farm on our left and Wall Wood on our right.

Our road soon bears right and on our left is the south western corner of Hatfield Forest, a remnant of the Great Forest of Essex, enclosed by Act of Parliament in 1855, and now, like Woodside Green and Wall Wood, in the hands of the National Trust. On the left we come to a gateway giving access for pedestrians and cyclists. Cyclists are permitted to ride the forest tracks with certain restrictions as indicated by notices and a whole day could be spent exploring here. Almost in the centre of the forest is an attractive lake, on which, in days gone by, one could hire rowing boats and many a cycling club would spend a happy summer Sunday afternoon afloat, sometimes to the consternation of the boat hirers. Cycling clubs were ever notoriously high-spirited! Alas, this pleasure is no longer available.

Beside the lake, formed about 1746 by the damming of the Shermore Brook, is the Shell House, an 18th century pavilion, its flint frontage decorated with designs in sea shells, where refreshments are served. Nearby in the seclusion of the woods is a former keeper's cottage which for many years was a youth hostel. A mile north west of the lake are the remnants of more ancient earthworks at Portingbury Hills.

However, if we remain on our road for something over half a mile we shall come to a junction where we double sharply back to our left. After another mile of almost straight, fairly level riding we dip down to bear left as another road joins from our right. Wriggling up and down around a couple of bends we arrive back alongside the forest edge and discover a small church peeping out from among trees, its square flint tower capped with a pitched roof more reminiscent of the Surrey and Sussex Weald than deepest Essex. A little distance ahead is the main entrance to the forest; motorists may enter here but they have to pay whereas walkers and cyclists use the forest free.

This is where those who have opted to explore the forest can rejoin us as we take the little road eastward from the church, dipping down and up again via the hamlet of Bush End. On the left facing the green is a charming thatched cottage bearing the unlikely name of "The Shambles". This may or may not indicate a bygone connection with the butchering trade, although the house next door was once a cosy pub, the Ancient Foresters, and the house still bears this name. Beyond, a stiffish climb takes us up to the B183, fortunately not as a rule over-burdened with traffic and a right turn will give us a downhill breather after our efforts before another steady ascent takes us past Barrington Hall for the gentle roll down into Hatfield Broad Oak. Here the first building on the left is yet another pub-that-was, the Fox, now a private residence, Fox Cottage.

The good news is that three hundred yards ahead, where the B183 swings right, is the Duke's Head, popular with Essex and Hertford cyclists for its sustaining lunches.

I am at pains to mention good inns throughout our expeditions as the tea places and cafés which abounded in Essex until about thirty years ago are lost to us. Cheap and cheerful for the most part, much of their trade derived from cycling clubs. Regrettably, few remain and unless we carry our own food and drink we are dependent upon country pubs, which in their turn are tending to dwindle in number, a trend disturbing to those who care about the traditional English country scene.

The name of Hatfield Broad Oak is said to derive from the Doodle Oak, an immense tree which once stood in the forest,

A picturesque corner of Hatfield Broad Oak

and the village grew up around a Benedictine monastery to accommodate kings and their retinues while hunting in the royal forest. There was indeed a move afoot at one time to call the place Hatfield Regis but nothing is heard of this nowadays and to my mind its current title is far more evocative of its character. The imposing tower of the church is a landmark for miles around and the main street of the village contains numerous interesting and delightful old buildings. It is therefore no hardship to loiter here awhile.

On our way again we take to the B183 once more, winding and undulating the three miles to Hatfield Heath, a spacious village with a large airy green straddling the A1060. If we omitted to refresh ourselves at Hatfield Broad Oak there are some good inns here, notably the Stag, again, popular with cyclists and particularly with local pensioners, always a good sign.

A few yards west of the Stag we fork left, keeping to the B183 which in a couple of miles brings us to the long straggling village of Sheering. It is worth making a diversion along a lane to the left by the war memorial at the Cock Inn to see the village church whose clock bears the sobering admonition "Work and Pray, Today is Yours".

Returning to the B183 we continue west to cross the M11, turning right immediately beyond it with due care given to sparse but fast-moving traffic. Care, too, is needed with the Bartholomew's map as it is inaccurate and misleading at this point. From here it is virtually downhill all the way to journey's end and as we drop down sharply to Lower Sheering we must be careful not to approach the T-junction at the bottom too fast. Turning right we find Lower Sheering straggling along the valley road like its upland neighbour and there is little of interest till we are entering Sawbridgeworth where, on the left, the distinctive and attractive architecture of the old maltings greets us. Performing their original function until comparatively recently the maltings are now converted into expensive riverside apartments and business premises.

Finally we reach yet another T-junction where a left turn brings us back to Sawbridgeworth station in three hundred yards. However, before we reach it there is a turning on the right which provides the alternative to the towpath mentioned earlier. This is a pleasant road leading to within a stone's throw of Little Hallingbury church - ignore a turning on the right after two miles - and if we fancy a brief waterside diversion, at the top of the stiff climb to Gaston Green there is a signposted cul-de-sac leading to Tednambury Mill, standing next to a boatyard on the backwater. Though it is now a restaurant the old watermill retains much of its character complete with overhanging lucarnes. There is a footbridge leading to the lock on the navigation but the fieldpath is liable to be wet after rain.

Note that when riding towpaths under British Waterways Board jurisdiction one should possess a permit. This is issued free nowadays although once upon a time a fee was charged and it can be obtained from British Waterways Board, Customer Services, Willow Green, Church Road, Watford, Hertfordshire WDI 3QA, or by application to any local BWB office.

Yet curiously enough, in many towpath excursions over the past fifty years I have never once been challenged and asked to produce one.

CHAPTER 4

Ingatestone - Danbury - Ulting - Maldon - Purleigh - Hanningfields - Ingatestone
43 miles. Mildly undulating to flat with a few stiff climbs.
OS Landranger sheets 167 & 168. Bartholomew's Leisure Map Essex.

This is another ride starting in Ingatestone which will show us a surprising variety of terrain and scenery within a moderate distance.

I have already mentioned rail access and car parking in Chapter 2 so we will commence our outing straight away from Ingatestone church whence we pedal away north eastward along the old Roman road, formerly the A12 trunk road. Once clear of the village we shall find little traffic to bother us since most of it now hurtles past on the bypass, a stone's throw from our left elbows. We can therefore bowl pleasurably along on a wide well-surfaced highway until within almost exactly a mile we can make a little diversion to the right along a lane to Margaretting church. This leads shortly to a railway level crossing beyond which continues a bridlepath-cum-farm road. The particular curiosity here is in the ingenious loading gauges on either side of the crossing, constructed, one of hand bells, the other of cattle bells, with the object of warning drivers of farm vehicles when their loads are liable to foul the overhead power lines. The church lies on the far side of the railway and on one of my recent visits harboured a large swarm of bees beneath the weatherboarding of its typical Essex spire. Incidentally, for those who are car-assisted, there is space here to park as long as one respects access and grass verges belonging to the farm.

Returning to the main road we could spare a moment to look at a cast iron milestone a few yards along on the right towards Chelmsford. This is probably a product of the Maldon

Ironworks and is set in front of a much older stone. The spellings show interesting variations on those currently accepted: whether these are old variants or due to carelessness or ignorance on the part of the foundryman is open to conjecture but perhaps it will serve to occupy us while we continue, dropping steadily downhill before a sharp rise into Margaretting. At the crossroads in the village centre we turn sharp right into Maldon Road which we follow winding downhill past bungalows and a few council houses till we pass under a narrow railway bridge. The railway here is the old Great Eastern main line to Norwich and the East Anglian coast. When I cycled these roads as a youngster the rural peace would be disturbed intermittently by the thunder and smoke of Sandringhams, B1s and Britannias, hurling expresses through with a flash of piston rods, a sight to delight the heart of any railway fan. Alas, they are long gone, displaced by gaudily painted, soulless electric multiple units, cleaner and more efficient no doubt, but lacking the appeal of those living, breathing machines.

However, enough of nostalgia and back to the present, as we take care on the blind left-hand bend beyond the bridge and follow our road as it winds gently on down through fields to the narrow bridge over the River Wid. Beyond and below is the constant hubbub of the new Chelmsford bypass, built to bypass the original bypass whose eventual inadequacy was exacerbated, as in so many other places, by unrestrained ribbon development. If we lift our eyes we can see the densely-packed trees of Galleywood beckoning, a prominent church spire lifting above. It is a stiff climb up through the delightful woodland and those of us equipped with gears will be resorting to large sprockets. At the crest of the hill a green opens out on our left and the Victorian church hides at the back behind a belt of trees.

Beyond the traffic lights guarding the B1007 we have to put up with a mile of unremarkable housing developments before we find a turning on our right signposted The Hanningfields. We follow this out into open fields until we reach a narrow lane on the left. If we turn along this it will take us past the Marconi works with its prominent radio mast, to Great Baddow church where we turn sharp right. Great Baddow's village entity has been largely swallowed by Chelmsford, but the village street up which we climb still retains a little of its character. Here was born the composer Armstrong Gibbs whose *Dusk* was often heard on the radio just after World War II and always evokes for me the rides I took then in the summer evening hush, now largely destroyed by the omnipresent motor car.

At the top of the high street we swing left over the A130 and then bear left again into Molrams Lane. In a few hundred yards, just short of a school, we turn into a lane unobtrusively signposted to Sandon. This is another quiet village in danger of being swallowed by Chelmsford and ruined by the ugliness of overhead power lines, electrical installations and the proximity of the bypass which we cross once more as we follow signposts for Danbury and Woodham Ferrers.

Ahead of us looms Danbury Hill, crowned by the village church standing on one of the highest points in Essex and a landmark for miles around.

Now a large and rather upmarket village, Danbury is of ancient origin, taking its name from the Danish settlement established here after the Battle of Maldon in 991. However, the site had been occupied from Roman times or earlier. There were military camps here, too, in the Napoleonic wars. For us though, in the present, it means a stiff climb up past the woodlands of Danbury Park, ignoring a turning on the left, till we emerge on the National Trust property of Danbury Common. From here we can get our breath while we look at the view southwards towards the low ridge hiding the headwaters of the Crouch estuary. There is a small car park here which we have found convenient from time to time.

Alongside this is Penny Royal Road which we take, still climbing, past the Cricketers Inn till we meet Mayes Lane where we turn left again to reach the summit of our climb at the A414 in the centre of Danbury. We go straight across into Little Baddow Road. After a level three-quarters of a mile past tree-bowered, detached properties we reach the General's Arms on the left and start to drop steeply down into the Chelmer valley, passing the Rodney Inn at speed halfway down. In my experience both these pubs have always welcomed cyclists.

At the bottom we come to Little Baddow Lock on the Chelmer-Blackwater Navigation. This is a pleasant spot and at certain times there are pleasure cruises available. There are also private boats and hire craft moored here although horizons are somewhat limited as there is no access to any other waterway except the open sea.

Dragging ourselves away from the waterside we continue northwards for half a mile, climbing gently till we reach a junction where we turn right. Continuing straight and level we could almost be in Flanders, wide fields stretching away from the unhedged, unfenced lane and osiers fringing slow-moving watercourses. In less than a mile we make another sharp right turn, downhill on a narrow lane with grass growing in the middle to where the gleam of water betokens old gravel workings between us and the navigation, now a haven for waterfowl. Crossing the little River Ter, about to lose its identity in the Chelmer, we enter a hedged-in section, poorly-surfaced on my last visit and where a sparrow-hawk, marauder of the hedgerows, sped on before us in the shadows.

At the end we turn right once more, through the quiet hamlet of Ulting Wick, and keeping right come shortly back to the navigation at Ulting Lock. Bartholomew's map calls it a canal but strictly speaking it is a navigation, being an adaptation of the existing course of the River Chelmer. Crossing the waterway we climb slightly for a couple of hundred yards before the 'main' road swings right and we continue on into another narrow unenclosed lane. Keeping straight ahead for almost a mile we find an even narrower lane on our left signposted Maldon. We turn into this and ride on until we meet a T-junction where we

All Saints Church, Maldon, with its six-sided spire set on a three-sided tower: unique in Britain

can see the tall chimney of Maldon hospital ahead. Turning right we come shortly another junction where we turn left. Crossing the bypass, occupying the trackbed of the vanished railway link between the former Maldon West and Maldon East Stations, we make a short sharp climb up into the centre of Maldon town.

In these excursions I have in general avoided towns but I make an exception with Maldon as it has always been one of my favourite objectives ever since my first ride here in 1947 when it was quiet and traffic-free and redundant motor torpedo boats rusted peacefully away in the Blackwater mud. Now the streets teem with vehicles and the trade in timber, coal and other commodities, which once kept the long-gone railway busy and was the reason behind the development of the navigation, is no more. Yet the town still retains charm and interest. The pleasure sailing industry has taken over as a prime earner - Maldon was long a boat-building centre, and a reminder of the old days endures in the survivors of the famous Thames sailing barge fleet based here for cruising purposes. Just off the High Street the salt works still operates - its product on many a supermarket shelf - and can be visited. We could spare a glance at the singular church of All Saints where a six-sided spire surmounts a triangular tower, unique in Britain, before strolling on the promenade for a whiff of salty wind coming up the Blackwater estuary and perhaps have a ride on the miniature railway.

I leave my readers to find their own places of refreshment here, Maldon is full of them, and ask them to meet me again where the road to Mundon branches off rightwards part way down the High Street. If we follow this southwards to the edge of town, ignoring any directions to the B1018, it will bring us to the southern bypass.

We cross this at a roundabout and ride on ahead across the flat coastland where Danish invaders inflicted a crushing defeat on the Saxon army at the Battle of Maldon. Ahead of us is Mundon Hill, a slight eminence up which we climb to find a crossroads where our road makes a slight wriggle. We turn into

Maldon waterfront

Blind Lane on our right and head for Purleigh church sitting square and dominating on its hill. In half a mile we are at the B1018 and, alert to fast-moving traffic, cross directly over towards Purleigh to turn left into a narrow lane within a hundred yards or so and bear right in a quarter of a mile. We soon come to the abutments of a dismantled railway bridge, until 1960 carrying the line from Woodham Ferrers to Maldon West. Even at the start of World War II the line was falling into desuetude and I clearly remember seeing, in 1947, almost its entire length being used for the storage of outworn rolling stock.

Beyond, we start the stiff climb to Purleigh and after the surprisingly steep pull will find the Bell Inn at the top, another watering hole popular with local cyclists. From this modest height there is a fine view back eastward down the Blackwater estuary as far as the bulk of Bradwell power station. Ignoring turnings to left and right, follow signs to Cock Clarks which we reach in a mile and a half, bear right by the junction at the Fox and Hounds to turn left at the cross roads beyond the village.

Another mile through open fields brings us to the B1418 where we turn left and bear right immediately to bring us into Bicknacre.

Entering Bicknacre we ignore the road to Danbury on the right and as the B1418 swings left we take the road on the right by a garage with due attention to the traffic, which is inclined to whip round this somewhat blind corner at excessive speed. There was once a priory here but Bicknacre is now little more than a dormitory village and after leaving its bungalows behind we begin a steady climb up through open country to East Hanningfield, an old village straggling along a wide green now hedged about with considerable modern housing development. There are two unexceptional pubs here, the Three Horseshoes and the Windmill Tavern, should we feel in need of further refreshment. Just beyond the latter we turn sharp right past a small industrial estate to drop gently down across pleasant open country till we encounter the A130. Bartholomew's map marks an 'improvement' paralleling the A130 on the further side but this has not materialised at the time of writing. This would have crossed above our little road but as it is we must keep a wary eye on the traffic as we double right and immediately left to regain our westward route past a telephone exchange on the corner. On the skyline to the left is the particularly ugly and obtrusive pesticide removal plant of the Hanningfield waterworks and it is pleasanter to look at the green embankment holding back the waters of the reservoir itself as we climb steadily towards more wooded country around West Hanningfield. At the top of the hill in the centre of the village we can turn aside to glimpse the reservoir but our route lies forward and downhill. We swing left by the Three Compasses to follow a narrow winding lane, tree-shrouded in a small valley, and emerge in a little over a mile in Downham Road. Here we turn left and in two or three hundred yards find Mill Lane on our right which will bring us shortly to Stock mill. This is a tower mill built about 1800, now handsomely restored by Essex County Council with the assistance of English Heritage, and open to the public some days in the summer.

Beyond the mill another right turn will bring us to the centre of Stock, an attractive village rather spoilt by the volume of traffic streaming through on the B1007. Turning left on this we need only endure it for half a mile, dropping down past the exceedingly elegant church with a handy car park before we bear right with great care into Honeypot Lane. Another right turn at the bottom will undulate us pleasantly past Buttsbury church, bearing right to descend over another narrow bridge across the River Wid before the last climb back into Ingatestone.

It is worth mentioning here that on the south side of the railway station lies Ingatestone Hall, sometimes open to the public and well worth a visit.

CHAPTER 5

Theydon Bois - Loughton - High Beach - Upshire - Epping - Theydon Bois.
16 miles. Hilly.
OS Landranger sheet 167. Bartholomew's Leisure Map Essex.

This is a short ride taking us around Epping Forest and over some of the roads which featured in my very earliest cycling explorations. A word of caution first: owing to its proximity to London, Epping Forest is a very popular excursion at weekends and holiday times. Roads are therefore busy on these occasions and I recommend doing this ride during the week if possible or out of season. The terrain is also hilly and some low gears will not come amiss.

We start from the London Underground station at Theydon Bois, actually above ground as it was once part of the Great Eastern/LNER outer suburban network and was steam operated all the way to Chipping Ongar well within my memory. Leaving the station we pick up the B172 westwards and climb gently alongside the green on our left where there is ample room to park a car if desired. At the upper end of the green we continue ahead past the church on the right, its copper-clad spire green with verdigris, to find ourselves entering Epping Forest, the largest remaining fragment of the old Royal Forest of Essex. On the right just beyond the church, prior to World War II, there was a small fairground, a retreat, as such permanent fairgrounds were called. This was on forest land and for many years afterwards the foundations of swings and roundabouts could be discovered, although recently I have looked for them in vain.

We climb more steeply now up Coppice Row, today just a commuter dormitory tucked into the forest edge. Once, though, there were two tea places here on the right as we climb, the Rosary first, little more than a hut in a rose garden, and further

The coal post at Jack's Hill, Theydon Bois

up, the White House, an imposing Regency building in which the almost legendary Mrs Hardy dispensed cheap refreshments, albeit sometimes a little unhygienically. Many an elderly cyclist will remember with pleasure contented summer afternoons in the garden here with bicycles leaning in the hedge and Mrs Hardy's tea and bread pudding on the table: now, alas, all swept away by bungaloid development.

Near the top of the climb stands a pub, formerly bearing the homely rustic name of the Wheatsheaf, but now known as the Sixteen String Jack, variously interpreted by successive sign-painters as a hangman's noose, a knotted whip and a musical instrument. Latest opinion attributes it to a local highwayman who favoured a jacket decorated with sixteen tassels.

As a small boy I once stood here with my father on one of his frequent walking expeditions and watched a cycling club come thrashing up the hill.

"Strain their hearts, they will, son," said my non-cycling father ominously. Somehow I didn't believe him and fifty years of much of the same treatment seem to have done my own heart little damage.

As the gradient eases we enter the forest proper, beeches and hornbeams crowding up to the road. In less than a mile we swoop down and up through a dip known as Jack's Hill. Here, in my parents' youth early in the century, when they came by horse-brake on Sunday school excursions from London to Theydon Bois, everyone had to get out and walk so that the horses could get a good run down the dip and carry up the other side.

Just beyond, on the left, we shall find a curious post standing lonely and mysterious. This is a coal post, a relic of the days when duty was charged on coal entering London, originally to finance the rebuilding of the City after the Great Fire of 1666, and is one of several erected on roads in and around the forest in 1861, all bearing the arms of the City of London and 24 VR in recognition of twenty four years of Queen Victoria's reign.

41

With our horizons hemmed in by trees it is almost a surprise when we emerge at the Wake Arms roundabout. The Wake Arms pub which gave its name to the locality was pulled down some years ago and replaced by a brash roadhouse incongruously named City Limits! The friendly little Fox and Hounds which stood next door has also disappeared in favour of a filling station. During World War II this crossroads was surrounded at some distance into the forest by anti-tank defences in the shape of concrete 'dragons' teeth' and deep ditches, against a possible German invasion. Why this particular junction should have been singled out for treatment in this way is anybody's guess and one cannot imagine it being particularly effective. These defences were not removed until something like ten years after the end of the war.

The famous Epping Road, though, is still here, albeit renumbered from A11 to A104/B1393. From the twenties to the fifties this was a favourite route with cyclists and at weekends would be thronged with club groups. With changing cycling habits, population dispersal and increased motor traffic there are fewer riders now using this once well-loved road. We ourselves will avoid its traffic by turning sharp left along the A121 towards Loughton. There is some traffic to contend with but it is a pleasant easy road. After about half a mile we pass a car park on the left. This is the site of a forest-keeper's cottage, grandly named Broadstrood Lodge, demolished in favour of newer accommodation a little further on, opposite Goldings Hill Ponds on the right.

Just beyond the ponds we turn right into Baldwin's Hill. This is a quiet residential road but the forest is not far away and as we pass the Forester's Arms on our left the view opens to our right and we can look across to the magnificently wooded heights of Blackweir Hill, its trees concealing the ancient earthworks of Loughton Camp. Down in the hollow is Baldwin's Pond, a pretty sheet of water worth a few minutes of our time. This was the old hamlet of Ash Green and we pass more houses on the right, some of traditional Essex weatherboarding, before the road swings sharply left and downhill - we have been riding on the crest of a ridge. However, ahead of us on the corner is a narrow way prohibited to motor vehicles. As cyclists we may use it, although a lady I met here was under the mistaken impression that it was a private road barred also to cyclists. Not so, however, and in a hundred yards or so we emerge at the Gardener's Arms, having avoided a sharp descent and consequent re-ascent.

We are on the edge of Loughton here and bear right down York Hill until we find Staples Road on our right. This is now a no-through-road for motor traffic but that will not bother us and we can undulate pleasantly along with the forest again at our right elbows until eventually we reach gates across the road. These are easily negotiated and on the right is Staples Pond, in my youth a respectable pool but now much overgrown and little more than a broadening of the brook draining down out of the forest on its way to swell the River Roding.

Beyond the second gate we turn sharp right into the steep climb of Earl's Path. This takes us rather breathlessly up through dense forest, past Strawberry Hill Ponds on the left, probably old gravel diggings, finally to meet the Epping New Road again at the Robin Hood Inn, a well-known landmark. Crossing directly over the junction we continue to climb less steeply, heading for High Beach. This is sometimes spelt High Beech - no-one seems sure whether the name derives from the beech tree of which there are many hereabouts, or whether from the sandy ridge on which the village stands at the top of the forest. All the forest minor roads around High Beach are now subject to traffic calming; there are sleeping policemen, width restrictions and speed restrictions everywhere; no bad thing in the light of present-day motoring misbehaviour, yet it brings with it a feeling that the forest is being 'parkified', manicured and managed in the cause of conservation. Yes, it always was managed, ever since it was dedicated for public use in 1882, and even before, but it was less obtrusively done, the forest retained a certain magical wildness which is no longer there and I for one regret its passing.

Climbing away from the Robin Hood we soon come to another junction. On the left is the famous Tea Hut. This has been here ever since I can remember - over sixty years - and has always been a gathering place for walkers, cyclists, horse-riders and, particularly, motor-cyclists. There is no cover, no seating other than logs, yet it maintains an enduring popularity.

Tearing ourselves away we bear right, still uphill through a 'pinch' to take a left fork which will bring us to High Beach church, the church of the Holy Innocents, bowered in trees in the depths of the forest. A right turn here alongside the churchyard will bring us shortly to yet another junction.

Opposite is Arabin House. It was in an adjoining house, long demolished, that Alfred, Lord Tennyson, came to live from 1837 to 1840 during one of his periods of reclusiveness and is said to have written *Locksley Hall* here. By a curious quirk of fate, John Clare, another poet of eccentric, not to say decidedly dotty, character was confined hereabouts in a mental asylum at precisely the same time. I can find no record of whether either knew of the other's presence.

Bearing right again we shall come in a short distance to the open space which is probably the most popular resort in Epping Forest, indeed perhaps a little too popular on a bank holiday afternoon. On the right is the King's Oak Hotel. This is where motor-cycle speedway racing was introduced to England in the twenties, on a track in an enclosure behind the swimming pool at the back of the hotel. In 1949 there was an attempt to promote cycle racing here and a race meeting was held at which the great Reg Harris was billed to appear. However, he must have got wind of the state of the track, completely circular and inches deep in fine cinders, and did not put in an appearance. It was left to a few London stars to struggle through the dust to entertain a meagre crowd, of whom I was one. As far as I know the experiment was never repeated.

Of recent years a conservation centre has been established alongside the hotel, throwing some interesting light on the flora, fauna and geology of the forest.

After admiring the magnificent view westwards across the Lea Valley to Hertfordshire with a glimpse of Waltham Abbey, our way lies down Wellington Hill directly opposite the King's Oak. Just where we start to drop steeply there used to be another pub, the Turpin's Cave, commemorating the famous highwayman. It had a rather smelly cavern of sorts in its foundations purporting to be a hiding place of the miscreant. I judge its authenticity to be a mite dubious but at any rate the place was always hugely popular with cyclists and motor-cyclists, chiefly on account of its cheapness - it was certainly not for its cleanliness; any self-respecting health inspector would have closed it down immediately in this day and age. Perhaps that is why it is now replaced by a smart modern bungalow.

Dropping downhill the youth hostel is on our left, the Duke of Wellington on the right, beyond it a golf course, before we reach a broad grassy triangle at the bottom. Turn right here along what is now called Pynest Green Lane, although I have a certain memory of it as Pynesgreen Lane on more than one old map. We are probably seeing a current example of the way place-names become corrupted with the passage of time.

With the forest on our right and attractive private parkland on our left the lane undulates and winds us along for a mile or so, our bicycles negotiating the speed humps with far less problem than the motor traffic.

Reaching another junction at the foot of Claypit Hill we bear left across the open space of Honey Lane Plain to meet the A121. There are pubs here if we need refuelling, the Volunteer to the left, the Woodbine to the right, before we continue straight across into Woodgreen Road en route for Upshire. Once a slumbering village its peace is now permanently destroyed by the constant clamour of the M25 under which we pass in a quarter of a mile. Just beyond the bridge is a building now occupied by furniture restorers. When I was a schoolboy this was a pottery producing earthenware flowerpots and the like. The place was never locked at weekends and I leave readers to imagine mischievous young cyclists wandering in to draw faces on the unfired pots and trundle about on the narrow-gauge railway which served the works.

At the end of Woodgreen Road we turn right into the long stiff climb of Horseshoe Hill, winding its way up past the Horseshoes pub and the church, to an open green on the left. As we start to descend we turn into Fernhill Lane on our left. The narrow lane soon divides, Fernhill Lane to the left, Long Street to the right. It matters not which we take, both are equally attractive and will drop us downhill to meet up again a mile further on. We are out of the forest proper now and a view of rolling hills opens up to the north. We cross Cobbins Brook and in a quarter of a mile the metalled road ends abruptly at Maynards Farm. Beyond is a gravelly bridlepath leading uphill between hedgerows. It is rideable for a distance with low gears but we shall almost certainly have to do some walking as it narrows and becomes overgrown. Those on mountain bikes will have an advantage as we take care to swing right after half a mile, for tractors and horses make the way hard and broken here in dry weather, something of a morass in winter. However, we can get through with perseverance and eventually come to a smooth green ride till we regain metalled road at Parvills Farm.

A mile beyond Parvills we meet the B181 on a sharp corner and keeping straight on can soon see Epping Upland church prominent about half a mile ahead. Our road wriggles its way past the church and just beyond is a turning on the right which will drop us swiftly down to cross Cobbins Brook once more. We now start the long climb up to Epping town, swinging right on the diverging B182 to climb steeply and then less sharply as Epping church and water tower appear on the skyline, bringing us at length out on to the Epping Road, B1393, where we turn right for a short distance to the traffic lights on Bell Common.

If this last loop through the 'rough-stuff' does not appeal, and admittedly it can be hard going in winter, we can use a shorter alternative by ignoring the turn into Fernhill Lane and dropping down through Copthall Green, under the roaring M25, and up through the forest again on Crown Hill. Near the top on the left is the entrance to Copped Hall, a ruined mansion gutted by a German incendiary bomb during World War II and never restored. Continuing straight ahead will bring us to the Epping Road opposite the ancient earthwork of Ambresbury Banks, by tradition the place where Queen Boadicea was finally defeated by Suetonius. Over-zestful mountain bikers were starting to damage the ramparts recently and cycling is now forbidden on or around the Camp.

Turning left along the busy Epping Road we rejoin the full route in a mile and a half at Bell Common.

It is a relief to escape the traffic of the Epping Road by turning down this road opposite the Bell Motel to swing right by the cosy Forest Gate Inn where the ceilings are so low that dart players must take great care with their trajectories, dropping ever more steeply past turnings to Ivychimneys and Great Gregories on the left, levelling out by the golf clubhouse - the greens here are on forest land on both sides of the road - before we tackle the short fierce ascent of Piercing Hill. As a boy I rode up this hill for the first time with two or three friends by zigzagging back and forth across the carriageway; the possibility of a motor vehicle appearing in those petrol-rationed days was remote. Fifty years later the manoeuvre is unthinkable.

Over the top, a long straight descent lies before us. Formerly the route doubled away to the right and back again, it is still there as an access road, but was straightened some thirty years ago in the interests of the speeding motorist; a curious irony, as the police now mount frequent speed traps on this very hill.

At the bottom we need a few more pedal thrusts before the final freewheel down to the cross roads at the upper end of Theydon Bois green and the end of this ride.

CHAPTER 6

Hatfield Peverel - Terling - Felsted - Pleshey - The Easters - The Walthams - Hatfield Peverel.
35 miles. Mildly undulating.
OS Landranger sheet 167. Bartholomew's Leisure Map Essex.

On this ride we shall see something of the plateau occupying central Essex to the north of the county town, Chelmsford, and a few of the historic and attractive villages hiding away in its remote fastnesses.

We make our start from Hatfield Peverel, principally because, if train-borne, it delivers us immediately into the countryside. For those using a car there is parking in the village, although there are stringent restrictions as in all Essex towns where commuter rail services are available and it may be better to start the ride from Terling, a couple of miles north-west.

From the station we turn right and head north westwards towards Terling, pronounced 'Tarlin' by older Essex folk, and climbing gently, soon find ourselves passing through rather park-like landscape. Half left through the trees we can glimpse Terling Place, an imposing mansion set in extensive parkland. This is the seat of Lord Rayleigh whose dairy farms surround the village and supply much of Essex with its morning milk. It is an unusual aspect of farming in a county largely devoted to arable cultivation and gives this particular area its distinctively lush appearance.

Losing sight of the mansion we arrive at a crossroads on the outskirts of the village where we turn sharp left. This will bring us to the centre of Terling, passing neat cottages and other buildings all obviously owing their origin to the Rayleigh estate. Following the road through the village we pass the main entrance to Terling Place on the left. The house itself is shrouded in trees and not visible from the road and is private, of course, although the gardens are sometimes open to the public and are well worth visiting. Passing a small Tudor manor house on the left we come to the green, flanked on one side by the elegant church and on the other by equally elegant cottages facing the long wall of the Place.

Having looked our fill at this very English scene we can retrace our wheeltracks as far as the post office stores on the left, taking the road alongside it. Dropping downhill we come to another green opposite the Rayleigh Arms Inn where there is parking space a short way along a loosely-gravelled lane, opposite the village hall. I also seem to remember being able to park on the green here on a bygone occasion, although it gets crowded here on a summer Sunday afternoon!

Beware the lane when riding, the surface is treacherous.

Pressing on beyond the Rayleigh Arms we soon run out of the village but before we reach open country again we might look down a road on the left where there is a pretty ford, a quiet and peaceful place to loiter a few minutes away, or at least until a group of one's clubmates comes fizzing down the hill beyond, as happened while I was ruminating here while reconnoitring for this chapter.

Regaining the upper road we wind along for three miles, ignoring a turning for Fairstead, passing the hamlet of Fuller Street, sometimes in open country, sometimes overarched with trees, till we meet a T-junction at Boreham Road.

We turn right here to tackle a long steady sheltered climb which, ignoring a turning to the right, will bring us eventually to the A131, an old Roman road, at St Anne's Castle, reputedly the oldest licensed house in England, though obviously in an older building than that now extant. Crossing almost directly over the main road we pass through a pleasantly wooded part of the scattered village of Great Leighs before swinging left and then right, following signs for Felsted. We shall notice on various signs the alternative spelling 'Leez', as often appearing on older maps; Leez Lakes and Leez Priory are signed thus and as we start a long climb across a wide exposed landscape we can glimpse the

Ridley's Brewery at Hartford End

lakes away to our left with the towers of what remains of the priory beyond. In Tudor times the priory became the property of the despicable Richard Rich, doubtless as a reward for his perfidy, and the future Elizabeth I lived here for a time, a virtual prisoner, during the reign of her half sister Mary. Although now serving as reservoirs the lakes were probably dug originally as fish ponds, to provide the priory with part of its menu.

Taking care to stick to the principal road, still following signs for Felsted, we arrive in a couple of miles at Bannister Green. The Three Horseshoes here is often used by cycling groups and was one of the very few pubs in Essex to open its doors on the day of the marriage of the Prince and Princess of Wales. This was like an oasis in a desert for the few of us who opted to spend that holiday awheel rather than goggling at a television set.

Beyond the wide green we bear left and in less than a mile meet the B1417 where we bear left again. Another mile of gentle climbing brings us to Felsted with its well-known public school making a traditional picture behind its playing fields on the right as we enter the village. There was a railway station here on the single track which once connected Bishops Stortford with Witham and, in the inconsequential way of railway companies, another letter was added on the station nameboard, spelling it Felstead, an error not corrected until 1950.

It is a pleasant place and there are restaurants and pubs to linger in if we wish but our way lies to the left just beyond the school entrance along Chelmsford Road, unsignposted as to direction but plain enough. We are still on the B1417 but there is generally little traffic and after an initial slight climb we are soon enjoying the downhill run into the Chelmer valley, very welcome after the steady climbing we have been doing over the last ten miles. At the bottom, right by the river itself, is Ridley's Hartford End brewery, built here originally to make use of the Chelmer water. This is still a family-run business, having survived in independence throughout the last thirty years of big brewery takeovers and it still supplies numerous pubs in central Essex.

Long may it continue. Although extended in comparatively recent times the original 19th century brewery building is still extant, complete with overhanging lucarnes.

Beyond the brewery we are in for a surprisingly stiff climb away from the Chelmer. Part way up there is a relic of World War II in the shape of a reinforced concrete 'pill-box' or machine-gun post: put here to defend the beer of Essex?

At the top we meet the A130, relatively quiet despite its expensive 'improvements' and here we turn right with care towards Great Dunmow. After a quarter of a mile we bear left into a minor road and shortly make a sharp right through the few houses of Ringtail Green. Turning left beyond them across pleasant open fields we bear left once more at Rolphy Green. The square, squat outline of Pleshey church has been visible on the skyline since we turned off the A130 and another half mile brings us to a junction where we continue straight ahead before swinging right to start the climb up through Pleshey village. The village was an ancient defensive settlement with extensive earthworks and a Norman wooden castle of which little now remains apart from the huge castle mound and a considerable part of the moat. Nevertheless, it is an attractive village and there are two pubs, the Leather Bottle and the White Horse, both frequently used by cyclists.

After the ascent of the village street we continue to climb, though less arduously, with wide verges on either side bounded by tall hedges. This feature possibly has its origin in the late 18th century at the time of the parliamentary land enclosures. Before the advent of generally macadamised surfaces a statutory width of at least 40 feet between ditches was decreed to allow alternative routing when portions of the carriageway became impassable in bad weather.

In a mile or so we meet a T-junction and, turning right, will find a pleasantly level road leading us to High Easter, attractive and slightly reminiscent of Felsted, whose large church tower is a landmark. The Cock and Bell is a good halting place if required and, at the time of writing, there is a signpost opposite made in cast iron by Maldon Ironworks bearing the name of the parish on top of the post, as did nearly all signposts when I first started my cycling explorations. There are a few others surviving in the county and for me they are a nostalgic reminder of those happy expeditions of years ago.

We are up on the plateau of central Essex now but it is dissected by numerous small rivers and if we bear left with the principal road through the village we shall soon be dropping smartly down, past a curious round house converted from a windmill, into the valley of the River Can. Undulating alongside the river and ignoring turnings to left and right we are soon at the foot of a long climb up to Good Easter. A narrow lane on the right just here leads to a long and deceptively deep ford which has treated numerous daring cyclists to a sudden ducking. We, for our part, after an interested look, will carry on up the stiff climb to the crossroads in the centre of Good Easter where the Star is highly recommended for thirsty and hungry cyclists.

The church here, unlike that at the sister village, is an elegant example of the typical Essex shingle-spired building and, again is a landmark, particularly from the south and east.

Leaving the church we head east on a gentle road through unspectacular but ineffably pleasant country, passing some of the old timber-framed houses so plentiful in Essex, and if we're lucky we may see thatching in progress, often by young men happily perpetuating a craft thought to be dying out not so long ago.

After a double bend over a stream we tackle a sharp climb to a T-junction where we turn left, soon reaching another uphill junction where we bear right and then left at the top of a short ascent, into a narrow lane. Two hundred yards on the right is the Fox, yet again a welcome for cyclists, and then another three miles or so of gentle pedalling bring us to High Houses on the edge of Great Waltham. We ignore the sign to the village and bear left into Bury Lane which will take us, a little grittily, down to a charming watersplash. We need not get wet here as there

The Street, Pleshey

The watersplash in Bury Lane, Great Waltham

is a bridge at the side and we can then climb up a sharp rise to a junction at the top. Turning right here will bring us shortly to the former A130 which we crossed further north. A new bypass to the east has freed it of traffic and, bearing right, we can roll peaceably into Great Waltham, a large and gracious village. Holding to the old main road will bring us eventually to what is now the B1008, formerly the A131 bypassing Little Waltham, now itself bypassed again. It now carries little traffic as a rule and we can cross easily to enter Little Waltham village. Climbing up the main street we shall find Brook Hill on our right. Following this brings us to Wheelers Hill, bearing left, marked as a 'no-through-road'. Being cyclists we can ignore this and on a small rise at the edge of the village will find a gate, easily negotiated without even dismounting, beyond which is a roundabout on the latest version of the A130. We go straight on beyond this into what is still Wheelers Hill.

Shortly we reach a house with a curious spired summer-house in the garden and bear right on Cranham Road beyond. We follow this, ignoring Domsey Lane and can soon see on our right the still extensive remains of Boreham airfield, a relic of World War II, now used, among other things, as a minor heliport and for motor trials. Reaching a T-junction we turn right, following the sign for Boreham and Chelmsford and soon pass some large lakes on the right, remains of once extensive gravel diggings and now an attractive feature of the landscape.

In another mile we cross first the railway, the East Coast main line, and then the frenzy of the A12. Beyond this we meet the old A12, now designated B1137, the Roman road we have come across elsewhere, at Ingatestone. When I rode this as a boy in the late 'forties it was virtually free of motors and now that the newer route bears the brunt of the traffic it has regained something of its former appeal. A left turn here will bring us in a couple of miles down into the valley of the River Ter and up again into Hatfield Peverel and the completion of our circuit.

CHAPTER 7

Stansted Mountfitchet - Thaxted - Finchingfield - Great Bardfield - Tilty - Broxted - Stansted Mountfitchet.
34 miles. Undulating.
OS Landranger sheet 167. Bartholomew's Leisure Map Essex.

In today's jaunt we thread our way through some of the quietest roads in Essex and at the same time see some of the most celebrated villages in the county - indeed, in England.

We start the ride from Stansted Mountfitchet where there is a railway station easily reached from London, and car parking facilities. The small town itself could occupy best part of a day as there is a reconstructed wooden Norman castle, a fascinating toy museum and a windmill.

However, our immediate object is to pick up the B1051 north-eastward out of the town in the direction of Elsenham. In a couple of miles, after crossing the M11 we reach a crossroads where we turn left, following a sign for Elsenham station. Apart from a short climb out of Stansted our road is level and we cruise past pleasant houses till we reach Elsenham station where the road makes a dog-leg over a level crossing; we ignore a turning to the left here. Just beyond the crossing, on the left, are some Pullman railway coaches standing on a siding, converted to a restaurant called, with some optimism, the Orient Express. More interesting from a historical viewpoint is that to the east of the station the now dismantled branch line to Thaxted made off across country to the north-east. This little line was opened in 1913 and had the distinction of having the highest summit level on the entire Great Eastern system at 402 feet, near Sibleys. It lasted barely forty years, closing in 1953, some years before the era of the notorious Dr Beeching. The private motor car and the fact that Thaxted station was a mile or so outside the village were significant factors in its demise. During its lifetime its air of antiquity made it a popular resort for railway enthusiasts. Regrettably, neither this nor the affection which it inspired among those locals who used it were sufficient to ensure its survival. Hardly a trace is now discernible at Elsenham but we shall see more evidence of it later in our ride.

Our road drops very gently downhill past properties immured in trees and hedges until the country opens out and we find a turning on our right leading uphill. This is our route but before taking it we might continue ahead, swinging left under a low and narrow railway bridge to look at what lies beyond, a 'village' of cycling club country headquarters, some almost palatial in a simple sort of way, a unique development of club huts used by numerous London clubs for their activities since before World War II. Unfortunately, the erstwhile tranquillity of the location was rudely destroyed by the construction of the M11 motorway. However, many cyclists still sleep peacefully o' nights in these cosy huts.

Having satisfied our curiosity here we can retrace to the road which leads to Henham, taking care not to confuse it with the lane to Little Henham, to climb steadily up into the village. As we reach it we find on the right the well-filled remains of an extensive moat, undoubtedly once the defence of a medieval manor house. Although on the OS map Henham looks little more than a block of housing development in fact it turns out to be an extensive village of thatched houses, manicured greens and ponds, whose character, quite rightly, is guarded jealously by its inhabitants.

We follow the principal route through the village, ignoring turnings to the right, and soon find the landscape opening out once more. Away to our left is a large telecommunications tower and we soon pass a footpath branching to the left aiming almost directly for this landmark. This is one of the few remaining relics of the Elsenham and Thaxted railway, for the footpath follows the track bed. In less than a winding mile our road makes a sharp righthand bend and on the left we find the trackbed of the old railway once more in evidence as the continuation of the same footpath. The line crossed the road here on an ungated crossing but there is no evidence of it on the right until we have gone another three-quarters of a mile and can see its overgrown embankment.

Ours is a pleasant road, level and winding across a high, wide landscape. When I last reconnoitred this route the air was filled with the pungent aroma of the rape fields, blazing yellow all around, alternating with the subtler scent of broad beans, this last so evocative of late spring in Essex.

As a matter of geographical interest we are riding the watershed of Essex now; to our left the streams drain into the River Cam and eventually into the Wash; to our right are the headwaters of the Chelmer, flowing south-east, at length out through the Blackwater estuary to mingle with the waters of the Thames off Mersea Island.

Through Hamperden End we come finally to Debden Cross with Debden Green half left, not to be confused with the other Debden Green, near Loughton on the edge of Epping Forest. We turn sharp right here between high hedges of hawthorn, heavy with may blossom in spring as if snow had fallen overnight. We ride a road unclassified but good-surfaced, climbing through Cutlers Green till suddenly we see on our left the landscape dominated by Thaxted's magnificent church, the 'Cathedral of Essex' some call it, although the title properly belongs to the far less imposing fane of Chelmsford. A finely preserved windmill shares the hilltop with that proud crocketted spire.

Dropping down and then sharply up again we find ourselves beside the church, an ostentatious reminder of the prosperous times when Thaxted was a centre for cutlery, a trade which probably fell into decline as firewood came into short supply; the bareness of the surrounding hillsides bears witness.

Turning right at the church we drop down Town Street to find the famous timber-framed and jettied Moot Hall, built by the Cutlers' Guild around 1400. It is worth a stop just to admire the

The famous Green and distinctive church at Finchingfield

harmonious lines of the buildings fronting the street, leading our eyes up to the all-dominating church. Those of us with musical interests can spare a thought for the composer Gustav Holst who lived in Town Street for a number of years. Probably as a result of this connection the church is used as a concert hall from time to time.

Throwing leg over saddle once more we continue forward on the B184 for a few hundred yards until we find a road on our left, opposite the ornate village sign. We turn into this and after half a mile or so of climbing past uninteresting housing we are in open country again and almost immediately bear left into a road signposted to the Sampfords. The lane is virtually traffic-free, even on a Sunday, and we shall probably have just the occasional kestrel or a 'charm' of goldfinches for company. Eventually, having passed well-surfaced farm roads on right and left, we arrive at a T-junction, shaded in trees where we could be a million miles from anywhere, so tranquil is it. We turn right and another half-mile brings us to Little Sampford church, almost hidden by lush foliage in summer, where we turn left into a lane signposted Great Sampford.

A quick drop down across the River Pant delivers us on to the B1053 where a right turn takes us up the stiffest climb on the route, Hawkin's Hill, which will have us reaching swiftly for low gears. Over the top we start the long, gentle drop towards Finchingfield. Unlike Thaxted, the distinctive church of Finchingfield with its Georgian-style bell-cote, does not dominate the landscape, rather it appears and disappears coyly as our road winds, until finally we emerge on to the green of this most famous of Essex villages. When such things were fashionable it was vaunted as 'The Prettiest Village in England'. Beauty is in the eye of the beholder, of course, and there are many other places with equal claim to that title, but Finchingfield thoroughly deserves its fame, containing as it does, many centuries-old buildings, including an 18th century windmill standing on the site of one far older. The penalty for its fame, naturally, is that the

Great Bradfield's Cage or Lock-up

village is rarely without its covey of sight-seers and for some of us its attraction suffers in consequence.

There is a good teashop on the north side of the green and some very adequate pubs. However, as we have now reached the furthest point of this run we might do better, having looked our fill at Finchingfield, to pick up our return route on the B1057 at the southern tip of the green.

A mile of the gentlest climbing will suddenly show us the mill and church of Great Bardfield away on our left shoulder. A welcome descent takes us across the River Pant once more on a very narrow bridge and as we climb up into the village we should notice the tiny old lock-up, the Cage, on our right. This is open to the public, free, on Saturday and Sunday afternoons throughout spring and summer. At the top of the climb in the village centre our route follows the B1057 by turning right into the High Street but we ought to spare some time to explore towards the church and windmill. Although a mite less well-known and therefore less crowded than its famous neighbour, Great Bardfield is, in my opinion, every bit as attractive, having a more spacious feel about it and containing elegant buildings in great variety, from thatched, white-washed cottages to Georgian houses and shops. The exceedingly handsome and well-preserved tower mill dates from 1661. It is privately owned and not generally open to the public.

Returning to our route and climbing up through the wide High Street we shall find teashops and pubs to cater for the inner cyclist, the Bell Inn in particular offering a cheerful welcome on my last visit. Beyond the Bell, further up the High Street on the left, is the Cottage Museum, crammed with displays of rural history and village crafts. Like the Cage, it is open on Saturday and Sunday afternoons, spring and summer.

Leaving Great Bardfield we are in for some steady climbing over most of the next three miles. This is open, exposed country with little habitation along the road, not unpleasant but irksome if there is much of a wind anywhere between south and

The remarkable church of St Mary the Virgin at Tilty

north-west. However, we eventually reach the shelter of a turning on the right, clearly signposted to Lindsell. In half a mile we reach the tiny village, its diminutive flint church hiding away behind the Hall, and ignore turnings to left and right to get to grips with some more steady climbing. Dropping down after Gallows Green we continue forward past a lane on the left and over a stream to climb yet again through Little Cambridge. Falling again we meet the B184 where we turn left. In a quarter of a mile we can see a considerable climb looming, half left. Thankfully, we avoid this by taking the next lane on the right to tackle the lesser ascent through Duton Hill where the great church of Thaxted is thrusting up from the skyline away to the north. Shortly we are dropping down into the lush valley of the River Chelmer to turn left at a T-junction and in a few hundred yards, right for Tilty, to start climbing again.

Just on the right is Tilty church. There was a Norman abbey here; those founding religious houses generally had a sharp eye for an idyllic location. However, little now remains of it other than parts of the striking church which embodies styles ranging from the 13th to the 17th centuries.

Leaving Tilty we pass a World War II machine-gun nest on the right and traverse wide open country, the houses of Broxted clearly visible in the distance. For companionship we have a procession of jet airliners on their landing approach to Stansted airport a couple of miles south-west. A right turn and then a left, signposted Molehill Green, bring us to Broxted Church End where residents' private gardens are sometimes open to visitors. We take a left fork here, confusingly signposted Takeley/ Broxted. In less than a mile we reach Broxted Brick End and bear right where the Prince of Wales Inn stands within a triangle of roads. The worst of our climbing is now over and, ignoring a lane on the right, we continue easily on to Molehill Green. This hamlet and much of the scattered parish of Broxted would have disappeared had not sanity prevailed over the original plans for the extension of Stansted airport.

Turning right at the Three Horseshoes we have a couple of straight, level miles ahead, almost into Elsenham. Away on the left is Stansted airport and, parked in their cars along an open stretch, the modern equivalent of train-spotters, plane-spotters.

Passing dense woodland on our right, once part of Elsenham Hall estate, and now concealing a golf school, we swing right to drop down and up again to the Crown at Elsenham. Turning left here we rejoin our outward route in a few hundred yards and so retrace to Stansted Mountfitchet.

Thaxted Guildhall and church

CHAPTER 8

Stansted Mountfitchet - Rickling - Arkesden - Audley End - Elmdon - Clavering - Manuden - Stansted Mountfitchet.
34 miles. Hilly.
OS Landranger Sheets 154 & 167. Bartholomew's Leisure Maps Essex, & Cambridge & Bedford.

Our little foray today takes us in search of the highest point in Essex, not, as so many imagine, on the isolated heights of Laindon, Danbury or even Havering-atte-Bower as some claim, but in the far north-west of the county where Essex shares the tail end of the Chiltern range with Hertford and Cambridge.

A brief word of warning before we start; although the mileage is not excessive we are in for some 'collar-work' and places for refreshment are a little sparse along the way, so it might be as well if we took something to eat and drink with us.

We set out from Stansted Mountfitchet as in our ride out to Thaxted and beyond, but instead of branching right on to the B1051 we continue north on the B1351 out of the little town until we reach the B1383. This is the erstwhile A11, now carrying but a fraction of its former traffic load, at least during the week. We turn right here for a mere two hundred yards or so before making another right turn into a narrow unsignposted lane which will zigzag us gently uphill to leafy Ugley Green, anything but ugly though its tranquillity is now sullied by the M11 just beyond. We pass under the motorway and shortly arrive at Elsenham railway station. We go over the level crossing and swing left to join briefly the route described in Chapter 7. Easing gently downhill we now ignore the lane on the right to Henham, likewise that to Little Henham, and with the infant River Cam for company, negotiate with care the narrow railway bridge. Perhaps we might spare a look at the cycling club 'village' described in the previous chapter if we omitted to do so on that ride.

Our actual route lies up the first turning on the left beyond the railway bridge and will take us under the M11 again, up a noticeable climb on a narrowing lane, around S-bends past Ugley church. In early summer the verges are creamy-white with wild parsley blossom but in winter I have seen the banks white with snow head-high, and the rideable carriageway scarcely wide enough for two cyclists abreast.

We emerge eventually on the B1383 once more, at the Chequers Inn, understandably a frequent haunt of the clubs with headquarters hereabouts, despite the often unwelcoming attitude of the former landlord. I have it on good authority that things are now much improved.

Turning right we come in a quarter of a mile to a little lane on our left into which we dive. Quiet and tree-shaded it will bring us in another quarter-mile to Rickling Green where the Cricketers Inn, over on the right, is a good place to stoke up if necessary before we press on directly across the pleasant green. Soon we are clear of trees and cottages and beginning to climb steadily across open fields. We can see the tower of Rickling church in the distance to the right and our road takes a sudden swing to the right, heading straight for it.

We swing left at the church and shortly beyond, take a turning on our right. In another mile of fairly even riding we are dropping down towards Wicken Bonhunt, meeting the B1038 at a T-junction. The village, such as it is, is to the right, but we shall turn left to find another lane on the right where a short sharp climb greets us before easing us gently down the valley of the Wicken Water towards Arkesden. At the edge of the village, in a mile or so, we bear right with the stream running along the village street. Like most of the villages in this corner of Essex, Arkesden has a good measure of picturesque cottages, many of them thatched, and is a happy hunting ground for the photographer or artist.

However, proceeding with our route we must take the next turn on the right, sharply uphill past the church, uphill until a

Thatched cottages fronting the Wicken Water at Arkesden

Audley End House; the River Cam is in the foreground

wide panorama of rolling hills opens out before us and we start the long swoop down to meet the B1030 on a bend at Clanverend Bridge. Following straight ahead will bring us in a mile under the M11 and to Wendens Ambo. Here an unexpected, steep S-bend takes us up past the much-photographed church with a row of thatched cottages leading to it. Wendens Ambo was once two parishes and the odd name is a Latinized form of 'Both Wendens'.

As we level out, a little breathless, we pass Audley End station on the left. Until 1964 this was the junction for the Saffron Walden branch: London commuters now drive from their dormitory there to catch trains at Audley End and the car park, enlarged across the former junction, is crammed in consequence.

Nearly fifty years ago, some companions and I, exhausted after battling a south-west gale from Bury St Edmunds, enquired here on a winter Sunday afternoon the time of the next train for London.

"Tomorrow morning," was the horrifying answer: and so we plodded on, learning that cyclists have more reserves within themselves than they realise.

A short distance beyond the station we meet the B1383 again and turn left to find ourselves winding down and then up again between the walls and woods of the Audley End estate. Topping the rise the stunning view of Audley End House itself opens out on our right, magnificent in its parklands behind the landscaped River Cam, the spire of Saffron Walden church rising beyond. The house was built for the first Earl of Suffolk, early in the 17th century, and is now open to the public from 1st April to 30th September, Wednesday to Sunday afternoons and Bank Holidays. There is also a miniature railway, often steam hauled, which operates on Sundays and Bank Holidays over a mile of woodland track.

Pursuing our course we continue northward on the B1383 for a further mile till we drop downhill past Littlebury church.

Henry Winstanley, builder of the first Eddystone lighthouse, was a resident of Littlebury. His ornate house was something of an exercise in self-advertisement, containing numerous mechanical tricks such as a chair on rails which delivered unwary visitors backwards into the garden to suspend them over water. Winstanley perished with his lighthouse when it was destroyed in the great storm of 26th November 1703. The same storm also caused considerable damage in Essex.

The main road swings right at the bottom of the hill and the cottage on the corner has been badly damaged on at least one occasion through a heavy lorry failing to negotiate the bend. Our route leads straight on, though, into a minor road which suddenly leaps uphill to give us a taste of things to come. Up we go, in low gears if we have them, around a left-hand bend over the railway and then straight up, on and on for over a mile. This is serious climbing but the reward is a spacious view to the right as far as the Gog Magog Hills east of Cambridge. At length we start to descend and the road rolls onward ahead across the open, breezy uplands. We go straight across a crossroads up a sharp climb before falling somewhat to another junction where we turn left, following the sign for Elmdon.

We are climbing again steadily, over a mile of it before we reach Elmdon village where we bear left, still climbing, to find the centre of the village where there is a pub, the King's Head, very welcome no doubt. On past the village sign we are now over the four hundred foot mark but we shall lose much of this as we swoop down again to meet the B1039 in another mile. Turning right we shall find on the left a narrow unsignposted lane in a quarter of a mile. We turn into it to discover it rearing up on end with deceptive steepness, trees and hedges crowding in on either hand. I have to confess that this one has reduced me to Shanks's Pony, and to reassure those who may be quailing, this is the steepest climb we shall meet on this particular ride, although we still have some more uphill work ahead.

Having surmounted this severe bit we level out to swing

right at the next junction, also unsignposted, and in a quarter of a mile bear left to climb steadily up into Duddenhoe End. There is a pub here, the Woodman, along a road on the left, with a caravan and camping site which might be useful for those of us who like to combine camping with cycling.

We are almost at our objective here, the road still rising gently around an S-bend. We are on a high plateau now and there is nothing to indicate we are on the roof of Essex other than an easing of the pressure on the pedals. Open fields stretch away almost level on either side edged with dark woodland, but we are at 455 feet here and there is no land higher in the county; we are well over a hundred feet higher than those commanding heights to the south east.

We fall imperceptibly to Langley Upper Green where we turn left, following signs for Clavering. The quiet road leads us through tranquil countryside with hamlets and little greens, an England which pre-World War II travel authors like S. P. B. Mais and H. V. Morton would still recognise.

Dropping gently we pass Bird Green and eventually arrive at a T-junction, where recently an elderly woman shepherding a pack of foxhound pups along the lane greeted me cheerfully.

"Lovely day for a spin", she called: 'a spin', an unfashionable word, seldom heard now but so precisely descriptive.

Turning left at the junction we hit a sharp climb crowned by two windmills, one on either side. Unfortunately, both have lost their sails or they might perhaps be as famous as the Jack and Jill pair in Sussex.

We now drop down a little snakily into the valley of the River Stort at Clavering. We can cross the river at a ford on our right and continue straight on across the B1038 towards Manuden. However, Clavering is a pleasant village with the remains of a castle and a spacious green and we might feel inclined to loiter here before pressing on.

As we are now following the Stort downstream we might expect some freewheeling but in fact we climb fitfully as our

71

The famous 32nd milestone at Ugley

road follows the stream high on its right bank and even after we are well beyond the Rickling/Berden crossroads where electric pylons stride obtrusively across the landscape we continue to climb until suddenly we dip to the left and roll downhill towards Manuden, hemmed in by green walls of foliage.

The long main street of Manuden winds between elegant house fronts of several periods culminating in the Yew Tree Inn, where we swing right by the church to climb gently out of the village. A short distance beyond modern housing developments on the left there is a lane signposted to Stansted and we turn left into this. Crossing the young River Stort, very weedy here, we climb across open fields till hedges start to close in as we bear right at Bentfield Bury. Beyond here we bear left at every junction through the houses of Bentfield Green on the outskirts of Stansted till suddenly we are in rural surroundings again, our narrow lane walled in by greenery in summer. Swinging right past a gravelly lay-by where gypsies sometimes camp we finally descend gently to meet the B1383 once more.

Emerging on to the B1383 we turn right and should spare a minute or two to pay homage at a milestone leaning a little drunkenly in the left-hand verge a couple of hundred yards to the south. This is the famous 32nd milestone from London, start and finish point of many cycling time trials since the early part of the century. Increased traffic has dictated the alteration of many courses and those using this road now start further north. Yet they are still referred to as the '32nd courses', there is a flourishing 32nd Association formed of the clubs making regular use of this road and the spot is so revered in cycling circles that more than one deceased cyclist has ordained his ashes be scattered here.

And so with the ghosts of those who have enjoyed these roads before us we continue south for another half-mile to swing left into the B1351 and the end of our ride at Stansted Mountfitchet.

CHAPTER 9

Hatfield Peverel - Heybridge - Tolleshunt D'Arcy - Tollesbury - Tiptree - Wickham Bishops - Hatfield Peverel.
35 miles. Mostly easy riding with some climbing.
OS Landranger sheets 167 & 168. Bartholomew's Leisure Map Essex.

This ride takes us to explore some of the coastal area of Essex bordered by the Blackwater and Colne estuaries, and the line of the old Roman Road to Colchester, now the route of the A12 and the London-Norwich railway.

I had intended to cover most of the region in one long ride, but when I came to reconnoitre the ground recently I discovered signposts conspicuous by their absence in many places, making constant reference to the map a necessity. This of course is time-consuming and I opted to split the coverage of this area into two shorter rides which could be linked easily if anyone so desired.

We start from Hatfield Peverel railway station and find our way to the eastern end of the village to pick up the B1019 turning right off the main street. This latter is the Roman Road we have met before. If we have a car there is a little parking in the village but very restricted though it might be possible to find a parking space at the further end of Church Road which runs south east opposite the church and curves round to meet the B1019 near the Wheatsheaf Inn. However, it may be better to park at Heybridge Basin, to be mentioned shortly, and start the circuit from there.

For now, we assume a start from Hatfield Peverel and head along the B1019 in the direction of Maldon. There is a steady traffic flow along here but not excessive and it is a pleasant level road, winding tortuously for the first couple of miles till it straightens out to drop imperceptibly towards the confluence of the Chelmer and Blackwater rivers on the right just past Langford church. Beyond the church a hump in the road denotes the empty bridge where the Witham/Maldon railway used to run. The tiny halt here on the right was named Langford and Ulting, although Ulting is a good two and a half miles away.

In a short distance we come to a new roundabout, so new as not to appear on the latest Ordnance Survey map, ostensibly placed to serve a new housing development, but I suspect designed with an eye to a future link-up with the existing ring road along the trackbed of the old railway. Bearing half right as a road joins from the left we find ourselves entering Heybridge amid a fair amount of traffic. Crossing the Chelmer-Blackwater Navigation we bear left at the roundabout just beyond on to the B1022. We cross the Navigation again - there is a very fine Victorian warehouse building on its bank to the right - to reach another roundabout where we swing right into the B1026. There is less traffic now, except on a Sunday, and we jog comfortably along for a mile, housing on our left and the masts of boats visible across the marshes on the right, till we reach the turning for Heybridge Basin on the right. The sign is on the left and shrouded in greenery in summer, but Basin Road is plain enough at the entrance. Another flat, winding three-quarter mile brings us to Heybridge Basin village where there is a large free car park clearly signed.

A couple of hundred yards more will bring us to the foreshore and seawall where there are two pubs, the Jolly Sailor and the Old Ship, both haunts of cyclists from time to time. Beside the Old Ship is the seaward exit of the Chelmer-Blackwater Navigation. This was cut some two hundred years ago as an improvement to the River Chelmer to allow the carriage of coal, timber, grain and other commodities between Chelmsford and the sea. The coming of the railway took away most of its trade and it fell into disuse and disrepair during the latter half of the 19th century, as did many another canal. Ironically, the railway has gone, outlived by its older rival which

The sea-lock at Heybridge Basin, giving the Chelmer-Blackwater Navigation access to the sea

Sail lofts at Tollesbury

now enjoys a new lease of life for pleasure usage. It is possible to walk or ride the entire towpath from Heybridge Basin to Chelmsford and I refer those interested to my article in *Cycling* magazine of 5th December, 1981.

Seawards is Northey Island, a National Trust property, and the stretch of water between us and it is Collier's Reach. We can imagine the collier brigs riding at anchor out there, grimy crews trans-shipping the cargo into barges for the passage up to Chelmsford, or perhaps just around the corner to Maldon for the ironworks.

When we can tear ourselves away from the nautical atmosphere, we must retrace to the B1026 where a right turn will bring us in half a mile to an unsignposted turning on the left, Chigborough Road. There are sandpits here, some worked out and now attractive sheets of water. We are climbing very gently, joining a road from the left, again unsignposted, to go forward till we swing sharp right at the next junction, once more un-signposted, till we can see the squat, square spire of Little Totham church, which disappears into its shroud of trees as we approach. A slight climb and a gentle S-bend take us past to join another road where we turn left and almost immediately right, with a signpost at last visible across the open fields ahead. Another left brings us to this welcome friend, pointing the way to the right into Beckingham Road towards Tolleshunts Major and D'Arcy.

A moderate climb brings us to Tolleshunt Major where we bear right out of the village towards Tolleshunt D'Arcy. Almost immediately we can see to the right the plain, square, unadorned tower of the parish church, built as are many churches hereabouts, within the demesne of the manor house. Tolleshunt Major's hides behind Beckingham Hall, indeed most older maps give Beckingham as an alternative name for the village. Another couple of miles across quiet, open country bring us to Tolleshunt D'Arcy, somewhat more interesting than its neighbour. We meet the B1026 again here at a small cemetery and turn left past the

D'Arcy House, Tolleshunt D'Arcy, home of the detective story
writer, Margery Allingham, for many years

church standing next to the moated Hall. Beyond, the road swings right through the village and our route lies along the B1023 to the right of the Red Lion Inn.

However, we might spare a minute or two to bear left for a hundred yards or so to look at a substantial Georgian house on the right, opposite a small green. For many years this was the home of crime writer Margery Allingham, creator of fictional detective Albert Campion. Her less well known work included social history and *The Oaken Heart* was set in this village.

Returning to the Red Lion we turn left towards Tollesbury and are soon bowling along a level road between open fields reaching away to the marshes lining the Blackwater, invisible from this low elevation. The higher land in the distance is on the Dengie peninsula on the further side of the estuary.

Entering Tollesbury at length we find a large square in the centre of the village with attractive buildings and a solidly imposing church. There are pubs if we need them but it is worth riding on beyond the square to fork left into Woodrolfe Road which will roll us down to the waterside where there are boat-yards and a row of former sail-lofts now in use as workshops for light industry. On my last visit there was a large lightship beached a few hundred yards out in Woodrolfe Creek. Unable to identify it I sought information from a man who obviously worked locally. Almost predictably, he knew nothing about it and cared less, a trait I have come across before but still find difficult to reconcile with my own consuming interest in things about me.

Tollesbury was the seaward terminus of the Kelvedon and Tollesbury Light Railway, built during the first decade of the century in an attempt to encourage the development of Tollesbury as a yachting centre and packet station. Unfortunately for Tollesbury, there were other places on the Essex coast better served by nature for these purposes and the little railway spent most of its life as a carrier of farm produce. In an area of antiquated branch lines this was one of the most delightfully archaic, but old-world charm is not enough in a competitive society, alas, and it did not survive beyond 1951, well before the Beeching era and hardly a trace of it now remains.

Climbing back up the hill to the village centre we retrace past the square, searching for North Road, a narrow unsignposted lane on the right. Turning into this we pass modern housing on the edge of the village and are soon out amongst farmland again. We ignore an unsigned lane on the right to curve left and climb somewhat to find, again unsignposted, the narrow lane of Colchester Road on our right. Taking this we drop down across open fields with a wide view on the right across the airy marshes to the gleaming waters of the Blackwater beyond. On the further side we can see the town of West Mersea tumbling down to the shore from the low heights of Mersea Island.

When I rode this way recently a Thames barge was in full sail in the estuary, one of the survivors of a once numerous fleet which, even into post-World War II years, penetrated deep into the muddy rivers and creeks of this coast with an infinite variety of cargoes.

Strictly speaking, the mudflats which fringe the estuary are termed saltings. For some reason the Blackwater is saltier than the sea itself and salt has been panned here since Roman times and probably earlier. In many places around this coast there are the remnants of mysterious ancient mounds, known as Red Hills from their composition of red earth, now generally accepted as having some purpose connected with the salt industry.

We make a sharp left turn to meet the B1026 on a bend where we turn right. On the left shortly is a golf course with a large and incongruous clubhouse in what I have heard described as 'Tesco Rural' style, one can hardly dignify it with the title of architecture.

We pass a sign proclaiming Salcott-cum-Virley - modern maps do not give it its full name - and arrive at a cross-roads. To the right is a dead-end road leading to Salcott village; the name is said to derive from 'salt-cote', a primitive shack in which salt-panners once worked. Unless we fancy a longish walk to the waterside there is little to detain us here, the pub marked on the OS map, the Sun, is now closed and after a look at an old chapel by the recreation ground with a plaque informing us that the village was mentioned in the Domesday Book we might as well retrace to the crossroads and go forward towards a wooded ridge rising ahead of us. Despite the reputation of the East Coast for chilly weather, these south-east facing slopes enjoy a generally warm, dry climate and have long been a centre for fruit growing; Tiptree jams are famous. For us it means a sharp, tough climb up to Tolleshunt Knights, a quiet, greenery-shrouded village where we bear right through the centre to emerge eventually on the B1023.

By contrast with most of the roads we have used in this area the B1023 carries its fair share of hurrying traffic but we have less than a mile of this, still climbing steadily, till we reach a crossroads on the outskirts of Tiptree. We turn left into Station Road, a reminder of the vanished Tollesbury railway; Tiptree station was just on the left, which will take us in half a mile to meet the B1022, another somewhat busy highway. In a short distance, though, we reach the Ship Inn on our right where we fork right into yet another unsignposted lane. Passing scattered smallholdings we reach Priory Road where we turn sharply back to the left and cruise downhill, hemmed in by high hedges.

We arrive at a T-junction by Priory Farm on the edge of Tiptree Heath and turn right for some more steady climbing, a tall telecommunications mast to the right, before we drop slightly to a crossroads, well signposted for once, to turn left for Great Braxted, where the Du Cane Arms is a recommended cyclists' watering-hole, and we shall doubtless be ready for it after our long bout of climbing up from sea level.

However, there is more steady climbing ahead as we go on straight through the village with views opening up across the undulations of central Essex to the right and to the left across the glitter of the Blackwater; up through beautiful woodland for a mile, ignoring a turning on the right for Little Totham, bearing left to arrive at Beacon Hill crossroads. There is a modern beacon cresset here, probably dating from the 1988 Armada celebrations, and at over 250 feet we can now see right out across the Blackwater estuary and the River Crouch to the tower blocks of Southend-on-Sea, some fifteen miles away.

The uphill work is over now and, turning right, we start to descend through the rhododendron-bowered detached properties of Wickham Bishops, more reminiscent of the Weald of Sussex than Essex, heading for the prominent church. This is a 'new' church replacing the old one, now disused, in the original hamlet at the foot of the hill a mile south west.

We swing left around the church and then right to drop swiftly down into the Blackwater valley. A mile of pleasant free-wheeling brings us to meet the B1018 on a bend where we go straight on between the brick parapets of a bridge. Beneath this once ran the Witham/Maldon railway mentioned earlier and to the left a line of trees marks its former course across country from Langford. Dropping down further we cross the Blackwater and if we look to the right just beyond we can see in the trees the unusual wooden trestle bridge which carried the railway over the river.

Another half-mile will bring us to a lane on the left which we take as the B1018 bears sharply right and then in a little distance we turn right into another narrow lane which will bring us out to the B1019 a mile south of Hatfield Peverel.

CHAPTER 10

Kelvedon - Abberton Reservoir - West Mersea - Fingringhoe - Layer de la Haye - Kelvedon.
40 miles. Undulating.
OS Landranger sheet 168. Bartholomew's Leisure Map Essex.

Our route on this ride continues our exploration of the Essex littoral between Blackwater and Colne begun in Chapter 9. It takes us through an area deeply affected by a natural phenomenon rare in Britain, the little-known earthquake of 1884; more of this as the ride progresses.

We make a start from Kelvedon station on the East Coast main line. There is a large car park at the station, free on Saturdays, Sundays and Bank Holidays and surprisingly little used at those times. During the week it costs £1 as long as one arrives after 9 a.m.

Leaving the station we turn right to meet, in two hundred yards, the old Roman road we have encountered before, just by the bridge over the River Blackwater. Kelvedon is a pleasant town, now mercifully bypassed, and there are some good hotels, making it an ideal base for a few days touring. The centre of the town lies to the right and there is little restriction on parking in the main street if this becomes necessary: however, our route lies to the left beyond the river for half a mile, into what is actually Feering, until we find the B1023 on our right. Turning here we drop down a little to pass under the bypassing A12 and shortly find a lane on the left signposted to Messing. It drops us down over a stream through a wooded dell before we start to climb gently on a shallow-sunk lane between wide cornfields. Forking left at the next junction we are in Messing village in just over a mile and swing around the church to turn sharp right at a T-junction by the pub. Another winding half-mile brings us to the B1022 where we turn left briefly before taking another lane

Layer Marney Tower

Canada Geese on Abberton Reservoir

on the right. Reaching a crossroads we turn left until we find a road on the right signposted to Layer Marney Tower which we may already have glimpsed across the fields to our right. At the next crossroads we turn right and ignoring a lane on the right, pass the few houses of Layer Marney village to find the Tower ahead of us.

Layer Marney Tower should on no account be missed. It is one of the most remarkable sights in East Anglia, a Tudor gatehouse built during the reign of Henry VIII by Henry, 1st Lord Marney, as part of a project intended to rival Hampton Court. By all accounts he ran out of money, not surprisingly, and what we see today is all that was ever completed.

At the time of writing the Tower is open to the public during spring and summer every afternoon except Saturdays. Admission is not cheap! The best view of the Tower is gained by continuing beyond to the church. This is actually the front and can be viewed even when the building is closed.

Retracing to the last crossroads we turn right and start to descend, keeping right. As a sharp hill looms through trees ahead we turn gratefully into a narrow lane on the right to avoid it and soon emerge at a T-junction at the bottom end of Layer Breton village. A right turn brings us up a slight rise and suddenly we find ourselves on a causeway crossing the western end of Abberton reservoir. Formed some sixty years ago by the damming of the Layer Brook, the reservoir is four miles long and is a paradise for wildfowl. Canada geese are here in strength and we shall probably see numerous cormorants, seemingly on the increase everywhere, as well as many other species.

When we can drag ourselves away from among the other bird-spotters we shall find a steady climb ahead until we turn left at the junction with the B1026. Within half a mile we turn right again into a lane climbing up past Great Wigborough church standing on its slight eminence. A gentle drop down through the village brings us to a left turn at the next junction, towards Peldon. Before we reach that place, though, there is a diversion we must make, just beyond the Little Wigborough sign, where a lane leads to Copt Hall and the church. A pleasant byway winds for nearly a mile towards the marshes, bringing us to Copt Hall; not a building but a National Trust nature reserve, and beyond it, the tiny church, reached through a gravelly farmyard.

Inside this church is the only recorded memorial to that earthquake of 1884, a brass plaque on the inside of the west wall of the tower, commemorating its rebuilding after the upheaval. Peter Haining's book *The Great English Earthquake* is a mine of information on an occurrence centred in this part of Essex, which caused a great deal of damage in the area, although only three lives were lost, as far as can be ascertained. The disaster was apparently hushed up by officialdom in the belief that such a catastrophe could not be admitted as happening in comfortable Victorian England, particularly at the time of Khartoum. The tremor was felt as far afield as the Manchester area as well as across the Channel in Boulogne and Ostend. It has been associated with a series of disturbances in Europe following the Krakatoa explosion of 1883. It was reported that the tide came in at Salcott Creek thick, black and stinking. Was this the first evidence of North Sea oil? Also in the church, just inside the nave, is a framed account of the September, 1916, shooting down of a German Zeppelin at Little Wigborough. The crew of twenty set it on fire before marching off to Peldon where they, apparently grudgingly, accepted surrender to a special constable before being handed over to the army at West Mersea.

On with our ride. Retracing to the junction we turn right towards Peldon where we bear right and right again at the Peldon Rose. This ancient inn was severely damaged in the earthquake when the chimney fell down, crashing right through the building into the cellar.

We are now on the B1025 and in contrast to the other roads we have ridden so far it is somewhat busy, particularly at weekends, with traffic for West Mersea. However, our interest is in crossing the Strood, the causeway connecting Mersea Island with the mainland of Essex, and we should take note of the danger signs here as, at very high tides, the roadway is submerged. Conversely, at very low tides the Strood Channel dries out completely. There is easy access to the water here and the Channel is popular with water-skiers.

Crossing the Strood we climb noticeably up on to Mersea Island after bearing right towards West Mersea. The town itself is nothing spectacular, although pleasant enough. It always appears to me like a piece of Hampshire coast set down in Essex; many people retire here, there is some beach, an interesting yachting centre, places to eat and drink, and an arresting view across the Blackwater estuary, the squat blocks of Bradwell nuclear power station prominent.

Retracing our wheeltracks back across the Strood we carry straight on at the Peldon Rose to stay on the B1025 for another mile and a half, ignoring roads on the right signposted to Fingringhoe Ranges, until we pass the sign indicating Abberton and Langenhoe just beyond which we shall find a minor road bearing away to the right. We turn into this and start to climb almost immediately, ignoring another turning on our right. Much of the land hereabouts is under the control of the Ministry of Defence and used as firing ranges. Public access is therefore prohibited. The warlike use of much of this countryside seems incongruously at variance with the peaceful lanes along which we are riding. Ignoring turnings to left and right we ride ahead towards Fingringhoe, the wooded landscape falling away ever more steeply on the left into the valley of the Roman River.

We go forward through the dip and over the crossroads by Fingringhoe church till we arrive at another crossroads. The road ahead leads to a private wharfage and that on the right to sandy heathland, much of it under quarry working. There is a bridlepath, though, around the back of the marshes where mountain bikers could amuse themselves for a while.

Our route lies to the left, along Ferry Road, and in a short distance it opens out a view across the River Colne before dropping us sharply down across the salt marshes to the water's edge. The ferry has not operated for many a long year as far as I am aware but the panorama of Wivenhoe waterfront on the opposite bank is worth the trip to this cul-de-sac. Wivenhoe was roughly the epicentre of the 1884 earthquake and Lord Alfred Paget recorded watching from his steam-yacht as the town was rocked in a wave-like motion; "The village was apparently lifted bodily up".

This riverside town has long been a boat-building centre - wooden minesweepers were built here during World War II - as has Rowhedge, just to our left beyond the mouth of the Roman River, where at least one round-the-world yacht had its origin. We shall probably see a coaster or two at the quayside there. Colchester, three miles upriver, was of course an important Roman station and those gourmets from the Mediterranean quickly discovered the delicacy of Colne oysters, famous ever since. Not so widely known is the high quality of the mussels also found here.

Turning our backs at last on this bewitching prospect we retrace up the steep climb, back over the last two miles until as we start to dip southwards we find a road bearing right sign-posted Abberton. This will take us into the village where there is a pub if we need it just where we cross directly over the B1025. There is a glimpse of Abberton reservoir to the left before we dip down below the level of the dam and make our way through the lushly wooded upper valley of the Roman River. Beyond the dam we start to climb steadily, bearing left at a junction for Layer de la Haye, leafily green in summer and with a welcoming pub on the corner as we cross the B1026, heading for Birch.

In a mile the road swings left, but we fork right into a narrow lane signposted to Stanway and after a dip down and up again across the upper reaches of the Roman River we shall emerge in a mile or so on the B1022 by the Angel Inn at Heckfordbridge. We turn left here, sharply uphill for two hundred yards, to find a narrow lane on the right, unsignposted on my last visit, to wind us along through fields and hedgerows, ignoring turnings to right and left until we reach a road on the left signposted to Easthorpe. Along this we go, bearing a little right at a junction after the Easthorpe sign, straight ahead until we reach the curiously titled House Without A Name Inn. We turn sharp left here into a narrow lane meandering past bean-fields and osiers till after some more gentle climbing we are in more open country and can see Messing church across the fields ahead. Once up the little climb into Messing, an attractive village despite its name, we turn right by the church and retrace our outward route over the last two or three miles back into Kelvedon.

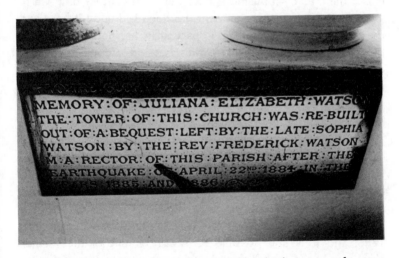

The `Great Earthquake' memorial plaque inside the tower of Little Wigborough church

CHAPTER 11

Burnham-on-Crouch - Steeple - Tillingham - Southminster - Burnham-on-Crouch.
21 miles. Easy riding with two sharp hills.
OS Landranger sheet 168. Bartholomew's Leisure Map Essex.

The Dengie Peninsula is that piece of coastal Essex lying between the estuaries of the rivers Blackwater and Crouch. Once upon a time these waterways were invasion routes for Saxon and Dane, but in my youthful cycling days they enclosed an area which time seemed to have passed by; there was no traffic at all and even more than the rest of Essex, it seemed to have been left to mind its own business in a nineteenth-century time-warp. Today, the hand of development has been laid upon it here and there and its northern edge, in particular, has become a resort for speedboat and water-ski enthusiasts with a consequent loss of former tranquillity and an increase in traffic on its east-west roads, notably at weekends during the summer.

However, we are still left with many miles of unfrequented lanes and the ride planned here is a relatively gentle amble attempting to give the essential flavour of a part of Essex which has a character of its own. The adventurous could extend it considerably, of course, and I have seen a road race of a hundred miles or so fitted into this corner of the county without too much route repetition.

Fortunately, the railway survives, having penetrated here in 1895, and it is still possible to savour a hint of the former character of the line all the way to Southminster. However, the service is sparse and for that reason, if no other, I have kept the mileage moderate.

I first came here on a day of high summer under a brilliant sky with a brisk east wind coming off the sea and a clarity in the air etching distant features sharply against the blue. I have been

90

The Clock Tower, Burnham on Crouch

back many times since in all kinds of weather but I recommend a first-timer to visit on a day such as I first did.

We start then from the railway station at Burnham-on-Crouch. Those arriving by car will find that there is free parking around the centre of Burnham and except at busy weekends there are always places to be found. Burnham is a fascinating little place and we could fritter the whole day away here, so it is probably better to do our ride first and give the town its due attention later.

Leaving the station we go due north, ignoring the B1010 on our left, passing the church laying back on our right till we come to a crossroads with a garden centre of sorts on the left. The road on the left is Green Lane and we turn into it, riding slightly uphill between scattered pleasant houses till we meet the B1010 in a little under a mile, coming in from our left at the Ostend George Inn. This road can be somewhat busy but we continue ahead for a short distance only, past the turning for Creeksea and around a right-hand bend till we find a lane going straight ahead on the apex of the next left-hand bend. This is our route, a quiet lane between open fields which will bring us in a mile to a T-junction where we turn left. Another half-mile brings a turning on the right and a similar distance along this will bring us to the B1018. We have been climbing very gently all the way from Burnham and, riding straight across, we top the ridge to drop down Mayland Hill to a T-junction at yet another east-west road.

A right turn here takes us up the first of only two real climbs we shall encounter, a stiff pull up through woodland until we level out thankfully to roll along on a pleasant open upland. In summer there are dog roses and mallow in the hedgerows and yellowhammers flit across the roads ahead of us. In our nostrils is that curious odour, like a mixture of seaweed and tar, which is the smell of ripening corn. Here and there we might see a field shimmering blue as water with the blossom of flax, a subsidised crop grown in increasing quantities in Essex.

A mile or so of this brings us to a turning on the left and we wind gently upwards along here until, around a double bend, we suddenly see the Blackwater estuary opening out before us as we drop smartly down once more to a T-junction on the edge of Steeple village. There is a pub here, the Star Inn, and a tea place, along to the left if we are ready for them, but our way lies to the right along a fast, well-surfaced road which, although unclassified, carries its fair share of weekend traffic, heading for speedboats at The Stone or Bradwell. To aid the pampered impatient motorist in his headlong hurry many of its bends have been 'improved' to leave a lay-by on the outer corner.

However, during the week things are quiet enough and a pleasant couple of miles will bring us to a lane bearing away to the right towards a church perched on a hilltop. That is St Lawrence church and we are now in for the second of the day's climbs - and it *is* steep. Unless we're feeling competitive a walk might be in order here to glance back occasionally at the view opening up behind us.

A halt at the top by the beacon cresset just before the church will show us the entire Blackwater estuary laid out below, from Maldon in the west, eastward to the ugly blocks of the nuclear power station at Bradwell.

There are always boats moving on the water and on one occasion I was fortunate enough to be up here on the day of the Maldon Barge Match. The sight of the Blackwater covered with graceful sailing barges is one to stay in the memory a long time. For many years also, during the ffties and sixties, there were several large merchant ships moored off Bradwell, idle and out of commission and rusting away into uselessness: doubtless those once-proud vessels finished up in the breakers' yards of Taiwan.

Having enjoyed the view and regained our breath we carry straight on past the church, of somewhat Flemish appearance, finding ourselves in a delightful lane which wanders along between fields and hedgerows, part of it forming a section of the St. Peter's Way long distance footpath. We part company with

Traditional Essex weatherboarding on the Cap & Feathers Inn, Tillingham

it where another lane joins from the right as we bear left around a double bend. Passing a wayside pump standing disused but picturesque at the corner of a farm track, another half mile sees us meeting the B1021 at the northern edge of Tillingham village.

Tillingham is a place to loiter in. Quietly picturesque, it contains many of the weatherboarded buildings so typical of coastal Essex and on a summer weekday still preserves a measure of that sleepy calm characteristic of all Essex villages half a century ago. If we turn right along the village street we shall find the square old church nestling among trees and two pubs, the Fox and Hounds on the left and the Cap and Feathers on the right, the latter a popular port of call for cyclists, and a little beyond is a far-famed bakery.

From Tillingham we could turn north to Bradwell-on-Sea, which is not on the sea at all, being over a mile inland and thence out to the ancient chapel of St Peter's-on-the-Wall, where some of us once slept in the pews during a night ride. I am told it is possible to ride the perimeter track of a disused airfield beyond Bradwell Waterside, a World War II photographic squadron base, and from there out on to the sea wall and right around the peninsula on it. However, I have no first-hand experience of this yet and in any case it is a very long way, so for now we will content ourselves with turning southwards along the B1021 to the southern edge of Tillingham where the main road swings right and we shall find Grange Road on our left. This is another delightful lane which will take us out on to the edge of Dengie Marshes. I last rode this on a day of blazing sunshine and I could see from this height of about fifty feet way out across the two and a half miles of green marshes to the glittering North Sea itself where the white sails of yachts gleamed. The landscape is not bare, though, and there are trees and hedges to keep us company as we gradually work our way round in a circle, ignoring any turnings on the left. After dropping easily to a mere twelve feet above sea level we bear right and start to climb gently. If the weather is clear and we look to our left we shall see a line of hills in the distance. These are the North Downs in Kent, beyond the Crouch and Wallasea Island and the broad Thames estuary.

In a mile we pass a little church in a grove of trees beside a manor house, virtually all there is of the hamlet of Dengie, which has given its name to the entire peninsula. Obviously it was a far more important place in feudal times than it is now. In another mile we pass the larger church of Asheldham and just beyond, the extraordinarily ugly buildings of an agricultural processing plant. We shall have been very unlucky if there has been more than one vehicle in the last three miles but we now rejoin the B1021 and turn left through Asheldham, heading for Southminster. Like many of the roads hereabouts it pursues a zigzag course, indicating in all probability that these are very ancient routes, beaten out around the edges of open-field systems and common lands, well before the days of the enclosures.

Other than at weekends there is little traffic on this classified route except at the end of the school day when fleets of double-decker buses bear pupils to their various outlying homes.

Unlike Tillingham, the pleasantly busy little metropolis of Southminster has many buildings in red-brick, 19th century in style and a result of the arrival of the railway. We follow the B1021, turning left into North Street, and then right and left around the church into Burnham Road. The church is old and severely Norman in style, reminiscent of the massive churches found in many French towns.

The B1021 will take us easily back into Burnham but before we enter the town we might like to pay a visit to Mangapps Railway Museum which appears on our right. Recently established, this does not occupy any previous disused railway but is a development on private land with over a quarter of a mile of track so far laid. It is open on Saturday and Sunday afternoons and Wednesday afternoons also in summer. There is plenty to see for those interested, including a working signal box frame, and refreshments are available.

A further mile brings us back to Burnham station but, if we have not already done so, we ought to carry on beyond to look around this attractive town which, of course, is one of the premier yachting centres of the East Coast. The town is full of hotels, pubs, cafes and restaurants to cater for our inner needs and, as cyclists, we might take particular interest in the Railway Hotel which bears high up on its wall the signs of the Cyclists' Touring Club and the National Cyclists' Union, both probably dating from the early years of the century. The most striking building in the High Street is the Clock Tower, erected to enhance what was formerly the Endowed School as a memorial to a certain Laban Sweeting, a local oyster merchant. Both the Crouch and the Colne, further north, have been famous for oysters since Roman times.

The river frontage is closed to motor traffic but we can cycle along it to admire the architecture of the houses and join them in gazing out across the fleets of small pleasure craft moored in the Crouch, an occupation hardly to be improved upon to round off our day in the Dengie Hundred.

The pump near Tillingham

97

CHAPTER 12

Rochford - Canewdon - Paglesham - Wakerings - Rochford.
35 miles. Easy riding.
OS Landranger sheet 178. Bartholomew's Leisure Map Essex.

Mention of Southend-on-Sea conjures up, quite correctly, visions of a large rumbustious resort with urban development spreading for miles around it. However, despite the image of this corner of Essex as the 'Cockney's Blackpool' we need only go a few miles into the hinterland to find pockets of largely unspoilt countryside, odd corners of which have as remote a feeling as anywhere in the county.

So in this ride we are going to seek some of it out, making a two-pronged foray from Rochford. There is a railway station here, on the Liverpool Street-Southend line and, although this once small and attractive town is now busy with traffic and beset with one-way streets, there is ample roadside parking near the hospital for the car-borne.

The town, incidentally, was the birthplace of the Peculiar People, a religious sect founded in 1838 and virtually unique to this part of Essex. In the main they rejected medical aid and were noted for living virtuous and honest lives. Possibly we could do with more of their influence in our modern materialistic world! However, enough of preaching, and a start from the station, whence we turn left to head north along an unclassified road towards Ashingdon. The first mile is an uninteresting plod through a nondescript built-up area but in just over a mile we find Brays Lane on the right which will deliver us almost immediately into open countryside. We ride ahead straight and level and as we pass a crossroads we shall see Canewdon church on its hill half-left across the cornfields. In another mile there is a lane on our left to take us directly to the foot of Beacon Hill, on which Canewdon stands. Almost opposite us at the junction is a road marked as a dead-end and we enter this to climb a little sharply up to the church. This is the only climb of any consequence we shall encounter on our jaunt and it gives us a chance to look back across a flat green landscape to the tower blocks of Southend five miles away. The view to the north from here is unfortunately blocked by the farm ahead of us but we can appreciate why the Danes chose this commanding height as their headquarters before the Battle of Ashingdon in 1016. The name of the village is said to derive from their monarch, Canute, who defeated the English Edmund Ironside in that battle. Curiously, neither the Ordnance Survey nor Bartholomew make any indication of the battle.

The way is private beyond the church, but there is a path through the churchyard leading to a gate on the further side where a tiny lock-up is tucked under a tree by the eastern gate. There is a tale that if anyone has puff enough to run nine times round Canewdon church - presumably widdershins - all the witches in the village are obliged to come to their doors: as well they might, if anyone were barmy enough to do it! Our road runs ahead through the village where considerable modern development mingles with much older habitations. Beyond the houses the view opens out northward. The low ridge we can see is on the further side of the River Crouch and Burnham itself is clearly visible. We drop easily down off Beacon Hill till we reach Creeksea Ferry Road running right and left. A mile or more to the left across the marshes is a marina on the Crouch whence a ferry runs across to Burnham, but nowadays only at weekends. However, it could be used judiciously to combine today's run with the run on the Dengie peninsula already described.

At the moment, though, we have other fish to fry and we turn right towards Ballards Gore. The view on the right stretches away to Canewdon church and a World War II machine gun emplacement sits oddly in the middle of a peafield, presumably intended to deter Hitler from emulating Canute.

There is comparatively little traffic on these roads but such

Typical Essex weatherboarding by St Peter's, Paglesham

as there is consists mainly of heavy grain and feed lorries and 4 x 4 jeeps whizzing about at alarming speeds in the hands of the bright young things who seem to form a large part of the population of these villages.

At Ballards Gore, the next junction, we turn sharp left and in under a mile, after negotiating a double bend, can make a pleasant diversion for a mile on the left to Paglesham Churchend. Tucked away at the end of a winding lane are some interesting cottages in traditional Essex style, a tree-shrouded church and the Punch Bowl Inn, well patronized by affluent pensioners on my last visit. Retracing the pleasant lane we turn left at the junction to continue eastward, ignoring farm roads to left and right till we arrive at leafy Paglesham Eastend.

Amid a little cluster of houses here is the Plough and Sail Inn, again patronized by the well-heeled, and they would need to be as, by my reckoning, the pub is on the expensive side. I offer no criticism other than that, but it seems that its proprietors are taking advantage of their monopoly.

Beside the pub a rough road leads for some 600 yards to the riverside. It is marked as a footpath but as motor vehicles use it we can cycle it with impunity into the boatyard which fronts the River Roach. There are warning notices about the locking of the boatyard at night but how this affects the legal position of a footpath running through it is not clear. At any rate, during the day we can find our way right down on to the slipway to look up and down the River Roach, edged by shining mudflats. Upstream to the right the skyline is pricked by the spire of Barling church, whither we are bound later. Directly across the river is Potton Island, part of the Ministry of Defence Proof and Experimental Establishment which covers almost the whole of this corner of Essex from Shoeburyness eastward. Naturally, the general public are denied access to the entire area with one exception to be mentioned in its place.

Having perhaps lunched in this remote resort we must now retrace the last two miles. This is no hardship though on a level road through patches of woodland and open fields: in fact we climb about thirty feet in that two miles, till we reach Ballards Gore again and go forward to a turning on the left which will take us through Great Stambridge. Swinging right by Stambridge church we shall see some large and unprepossessing buildings to the left. These are grain mills on the Roach and although we pass a road leading to them there is no riverside access for the public that way. However, since making my last reconnoitre, close scrutiny of the OS map reveals what may be a bridlepath wriggling around the side of the mills to finish up on the B1013 south of Rochford, thus dodging some of that town's traffic-ridden streets. Without personal knowledge, though, I must leave the adventurous to investigate for themselves. For the moment we must brave the hubbub of Rochford, bearing left at every junction till we meet the B1013. This is busy and we turn left with the traffic for half a mile to a roundabout. Southend airport is just to our right here, beyond the railway, but there is little to be seen of it on account of high hedges. Nevertheless, those of us interested in aircraft will already have noticed a variety of vintage machines coming and going at low altitude. There are no large jetliners flying from here and unfortunately the converted vehicle-carrying DC4s no longer operate the Channel Air Bridge to Ostend and Le Touquet.

At the roundabout we turn left but will have to bear with a modicum of traffic until we pass the Sutton industrial area and then dive gratefully into a lane on the left on a right-hand bend, signposted to Barling and the Wakerings. All is peace once more and we dogleg our way along for a couple of miles until we reach a junction where we turn left to enter the hamlet of Stonebridge, and almost immediately left again. We are now within the purlieus of Barling, which regards itself as the upmarket village of the Southend hinterland. True, there are pleasant houses scattered along the winding road until we find Mucking Hall Lane to our left to take us to Barling church. The route through the village is shorter but this way is delightful, a level narrow lane quietly making its way across wide fields, along by hedgerows to the church, clearly visible first on our right and then ahead as the lane makes a right-angle turn. We cross a broad private road, used by heavy lorries, which is so recent it does not appear on even the most recent OS map.

At Barling church we swing right around on ourselves and then bear left at the next junction into Little Wakering. This is a long, straggling village of hotch-potch development, modern houses cheek by jowl with older buildings, and now runs practically without break into Great Wakering, which starts where we turn left at the next T-junction on to the B1017. When I first rode this way forty-five years ago Great Wakering was still very much a country village. Today Southend has reached out and touched it with a finger of development without uplifting it in any way and like Little Wakering it is a melange lacking character and breathing a faint air of seediness.

We ride right through the main street to bear right by the church and almost immediately left into a road signposted Foulness. This is misleading as we cannot go to Foulness, the largest island on the Essex coast; it has not been possible within my recollection as it is wholly within the experimental establishment mentioned earlier. Its name, pronounced with the accent on the second syllable, means 'promontory of birds', the extensive Maplin and Foulness Sands fringing it, hosting thousands of wildfowl of many species. We can, however, ride at least another mile as far as Samuels Corner, the entry to the MoD enclave. Police will stop us if we attempt to go further along the Foulness road and if red flags are flying this is the limit of our exploration. If firing is not in progress, though, there will be no flags hoisted and we shall be allowed to go as far as Wakering Stairs, the start of the Broomway, a causeway uncovered at low tide which runs out across the Maplin Sands a quarter of a mile or so offshore for five miles along the coast of Foulness Island. It takes its name from the besom-like markers which used to indicate its course. Of its original purpose I can only hazard a guess that it was possibly connected with the gathering of shellfish. Unfortunately, we shall have to take pot-luck on this diversion as there is no way of knowing precisely when firing will or will not be in progress, although the police on the gate are usually quite helpful and evenings and weekends are probably a safer bet.

Maplin, of course, was a proposed site for the third London airport. It was dropped ostensibly because it was held the large numbers of birds hereabouts would be a danger to aircraft. My own private view is that the Ministry of Defence did not want any disturbance to whatever deadly projects they have under wraps at Foulness. When I first came here in 1950 there were huge ring-like structures as high as electricity pylons in a row two or three miles long, looking very mysterious and menacing. I assume they were for measuring trajectory and velocity of projectiles. They have long since disappeared, doubtless superseded by more sophisticated technology.

Returning to Great Wakering it is worth noting that the Anchor Inn is open all day for our refreshment if required before we press on, retracing rightwards into Little Wakering until we reach Barrow Hall Road on our left in about a quarter of a mile. Immediately we are back in rural solitude, climbing imperceptibly across the broad new private road, only the tower blocks of Southend on the southern horizon reminding us that we are not a hundred miles from anywhere. Completing our circuit back to Stonebridge we bear left and then right to retrace the last three miles back into Rochford.

CHAPTER 13

Kelvedon - Coggeshall - Castle Hedingham - Halstead - Earls
Colne - Kelvedon.
42 Miles. Undulating to moderately hilly.
OS Landranger sheets 154, 155, 167 & 168. Bartholomew's
Leisure Map Essex.

Here we are again at Kelvedon station, this time to see
something of the upper Colne valley, rather different in
character from its seaward reaches which occupied us for part
of Chapter 10. We start as before by turning right out of the
station yard to join the B1024, the old Roman road running
through the centre of the town. There was a Roman station
here and the OS map reminds us of its name, Canonium. We
turn left over the River Blackwater and passing the B1023 on the
right which we used previously, look for the next turning on our
left, not to be confused with the road immediately opposite the
B1023 which leads nowhere.

Having found our turning we pass under the railway again
and up through Feering village, bearing left by the church and out
into open countryside, on an easy road heading for Coggeshall,
the Blackwater winding along in the valley to our left. In a couple
of gentle miles we meet the Roman road of Stane Street running
east-west between Colchester and Ermine Street at Puckeridge,
thirty miles away across the Hertfordshire border.

Once heavily trafficked, this part of Stane Street is now
bypassed and we can turn left comfortably and then almost
immediately right into the outskirts of Coggeshall. This a
charming little town which we shall have a good look at on our
way back. For the moment we go forward until we meet a road
bearing right, signposted to Earls Colne. Within a hundred yards
or so we branch right again into a road alongside the Alexandra
Inn, marked as a dead-end. Curiously, authority has not seen fit

to remove the speed de-restriction sign which we shall pass near the end of the houses, shortly before the road becomes a footpath for a few yards!

Beyond this we shall find the new bypass whose speeding traffic demands a good deal of respect as we cross directly over into the unsignposted lane continuing ahead. We now climb easily for a mile, bearing right at the next junction. This is a gentle upland of smiling cornfields and after bearing left at the next T-junction we wind along towards the square tower of Great Tey church. We turn right at another T-junction, into the village to arrive at the church. The building is worth a glance for its massive Norman style tower with rounded arches before we turn sharp left and climb steadily once more. Through Swan Street we start to drop quite sharply and will soon see the soaring arches of Chappel viaduct, built in the mid-19th century, nearly a quarter of a mile long and the most impressive piece of railway architecture in East Anglia.

Happily, it still carries trains as the Stour Valley line is still open from Marks Tey to Sudbury, made viable by a considerable commuter traffic from the latter town. Nearly fifty years ago, during my service in the RAF, I travelled this line right through to Bury St Edmunds in an antiquated coach with odd little seats tucked away behind the corridor connection, hauled by an equally antiquated steam locomotive which was forced to halt more than once through cows wandering on the line.

In those days one could get all over East Anglia by train, given time, that is; today we are left with a few truncated remnants supported by a tenuous passenger custom while the once remunerative freight traffic thunders its way along our overcrowded roads in obscenely huge lorries.

However, crossing the busy A604 and climbing sharply for a quarter of a mile we can indulge our nostalgia at Chappel and Wakes Colne station just on the right for, besides still being a working station serving the local community, it also houses the East Anglian Railway Museum. The museum covers a four acre

Chappel Viaduct

The circular Templars church at Little Maplestead

site and is open every day of the year, with steam and diesel operations on the first Sunday monthly.

Continuing on our way we level out and soon cross a humpbacked bridge, which carried the road over the metals of the now vanished Colne Valley Railway. This left the Stour Valley line here on a more direct route for Cambridge via Haverhill. At the time of writing the trackbed to the right is occupied by an ostrich farm. We shall see more of the CVR later in our ride.

Past the bridge we look for the first turning on the left to take us through Wakes Colne Green to a right turn, followed quickly by a left into a lane meandering easily through the cornfields. Passing directly over the next crossroads we continue this delightful byway, sometimes tree-shaded, sometimes open, ignoring turnings on the right signposted to Daw's Cross - many of the signposts hereabouts are much overgrown by hedges - until we reach the hamlet of Countess Cross. We turn right here and in a little over two miles reach a triangular junction on the edge of Pebmarsh. Now a quiet dormitory the village has its claim to fame as the place where Samuel Courtauld started the silk farming business which was to make him a world-wide household name before the business suddenly went to the wall in the last decade of this century. As the industry grew he moved it to nearby Halstead with its ready workforce and rail access and was in a large measure responsible for the onward growth of that town.

Swinging left we drop down through Pebmarsh and will find the King's Head conveniently situated at the foot of the hill before we start the climb up the other side to cross the A131 in two more miles. Following signs for Castle Hedingham we bear right and left through Little Maplestead, noting the Templars' church on the left built of flint in circular form. Half-right we shall soon see the church of Great Maplestead and at the foot of a downhill run will find a turning on our right leading up through the pleasant village. As we level out the view opens out ahead and we can see the bulk of Castle Hedingham itself rising above the trees in the distance. In a short while we meet the B1058 and turn left to drop increasingly steeply down into Castle Hedingham village. Why it should be called Castle Hedingham rather than Hedingham Castle is a moot point, possibly from a Norman French precedent, but to my ear it has a more sonorous and commanding ring to it in the form used.

At the edge of the village we bear right into Bayley Street and will find the castle entrance just along on the right. Unfortunately for those interested in photographing or drawing the castle it is not possible to see it from the village and to get close to it one has to pay even to enter the grounds, let alone the castle itself. Only the 100' high keep now remains of a castle built in the 12th century by the Earls of Oxford to dominate the Colne valley. The village has many ancient and interesting buildings as well as a comprehensively stocked cycle shop whose proprietor conducts a thriving mail order business all over Britain.

Beyond the village we meet the A604 again. Our route lies up the steep lane ahead but, although the A604 carries too much traffic for pleasurable cycling, it is worth diverting half a mile to the right to the Colne Valley Railway preservation centre. The station building here is authentic Colne Valley Railway, originally at Sible Hedingham, a mile away, and has been rebuilt at the centre brick by brick. The centre is open daily from March to December with steam in operation every Sunday from the end of March to October over nearly a mile of track. It is worth remembering that the restaurant, housed in a railway coach, is open every day during this period and offers excellent catering.

Returning to our route we climb the steep, narrow lane aforementioned till we reach Highstreet Green where we turn left to climb still more to a right turn at a T-junction. A tree-shaded lane will bring us in tranquillity to yet another T-junction - we shall have little company in these lanes other than birds and butterflies - and, after turning left, a further slight ascent through open fields brings us to a crossroads. We go straight across here, heading for Blackmore End, despite the signpost indicating it to the right, and a winding mile through woods and plantations will bring us to the short climb up into the small village.

A left turn sets us on the road to Beazley End, a zigzag mile up a slight gradient, and we might well see fit to make use of the Cock Inn here after the sessions of climbing we have put in. We are in Grand Prix of Essex country here and the traditional route of this long-established race takes competitors up the hill below the Cock several times, no wonder it becomes christened 'Beastly End'.

Our route, though, turns left and a pleasant roads swings us along for a couple of miles till we ease downhill to cross the end of Gosfield Lake, formed by damming the Bourne Brook, a tributary of the Colne. The lake is popular with anglers and water-skiers and on a busy Sunday can be more reminiscent of Southend than rural Essex. However, it is undeniably pleasant and there are camping facilities here, too.

In Gosfield village we meet the A1017 to turn left and then right in a few hundred yards towards Halstead. This road will dip us up and down past a turning on the right, which we ignore, before swinging right to drop us down into Halstead town beside a large church with a spire. We turn left to drop on down the hill, swinging right at the bottom to cross the Colne with the bus station on our right, formerly the railway station, closed in 1962, a little over a century after the line was opened. Bartholomew's map still marks a level crossing on the corner although it is long gone.

Around to the left we start the climb of the steep High Street, long famous among cyclists as the finishing stretch of the Grand Prix of Essex. For over forty years a Sunday in late March has seen High Street thronged with clubfolk anxious to cheer their favourites up the last punishing yards of the 90 mile Grand Prix. Bereft of race razzmatazz Halstead presents an air of solid prosperity, perhaps a veneer in the present economic climate but a hangover from the days of Courtauld's prosperity and the town's rôle as the headquarters of the Colne Valley Railway.

There are plenty of places for food and drink here if necessary. We continue afterwards up to the top of the High Street, passing junctions to left and right, climbing ahead until we find Colne Road on the right. This has speed humps for a quarter of a mile but these need not worry us and we go ahead to drop down towards a small industrial complex.

There is a turning on the left to Colne Engaine. Dropping fast as we are with our attention on the road and the signpost unobtrusive on the right it is very easy to miss! Once found, we climb steadily again until we are bowling along a level upland road, the Colne Valley falling away on our right. A sharp dip and climb bring us through Colne Engaine village to a junction by the church where we turn right down the steep hill of Station Road, yet another legacy of the vanished railway. At the foot of the hill we cross the Colne, meandering lazily through lush water-meadows and just beyond, on the left, the building which was Earls Colne station is still recognizable as part of a private works. We now face a hard long climb, steep at first, up into the little town of Earls Colne. Once again we encounter the A604, turning left, but only for a few yards as we are going to turn right into Foundry Lane. The origin of the name is obvious as on our right is the Victorian redbrick of the foundry itself, once a producer of agricultural machinery and implements and all along the street are the redbrick cottages built for foundry workers.

At the end of Foundry Lane we turn right into Hay House Lane and are immediately in the country again. In a quarter of a mile we take a lane on the left, climbing a little and winding along until we can discern the remains of Earls Colne airfield on the right. This was used at least once for cycle racing within quite recent times but is now given over to light industry and a golf course. As we meet the B1024 there is a military type Nissen hut on the left which in all probability was the guardroom for this makeshift wartime airstrip.

A right turn and three uneventful miles bring us to the Coggeshall bypass. We cross this right and then left to continue ahead into Coggeshall town and in less than half a mile reach the Alexandra Inn once more. Passing it we bear right now to ride through the centre of the town, a treasure house of handsome buildings of several periods; so much so that any artist or photographer is spoilt for choice. One of its most attractive features is a small clock tower at the lower end of the High Street, just before we reach Stane Street. The most famous is Paycocke's, a medieval merchant's house, much restored, in the care of the National Trust and open to the public.

Coggeshall deserves a lot of time devoted to it, but for now we shall turn right briefly on Stane Street and then left, following the B1024, although we might loiter a while on the bridge over the Blackwater which is most attractive here. The road lifts sharply up to Coggeshall Hamlet, but this is the last climb of the day and our last couple of miles is an easy amble back to our starting point at Kelvedon.

The East Anglian Railway Museum at Wake's Colne & Chappel Station

CHAPTER 14

Newport - Saffron Walden - Hempstead - Steeple Bumpstead - Radwinter - Newport.
34 miles. Hilly.
OS Landranger 154 & 167. Bartholomew's Leisure Maps Essex, and Cambridge & Bedford.

As we discovered in Chapter 8, Essex can present us with some demanding climbing in its north-western corner and in our penultimate route we shall tackle some more of it, this time on the eastern side of the London-Norwich highway, the old A11.

We make our start from Newport, a large and attractive village stretched along what is now the B1383. In the days of horse-drawn transport it would have been a staging post on the journey from London to Cambridge or Norwich, as evidenced by the Coach and Horses Inn, one of the few pubs in which one could get a roast Sunday dinner in the late 'forties. There is also a railway station to suit our convenience, served from Liverpool Street. It has a large car-park, quite cheap, although on Sundays there is adequate parking in Station Road. This would not be the case during the week but a judicious exploration of byways on either side of the main road will find spots where a car can be left safely for a few hours.

So we leave the station on the west side along Station Road, meeting the B1383 in two hundred yards to turn right. In a short distance we turn right again into a road signposted to Debden and Carver Barracks. It is also designated as an alternative route northwards to avoid the low railway bridge at the north end of the village. However, it does not seem much used nowadays as most heavy loads use the M11 motorway. Crossing a hump-backed bridge over the railway we start to climb sharply and shall continue to climb for over a mile into open country, bearing left at the first junction. A sharp drop takes us past the

Market Square, Saffron Walden

trees of Debden Park on the right; there is a lake here, quite near the road, but during summer at least it is completely screened from our view by dense tree growth.

Climbing again we reach a crossroads, turning left to climb yet more, winding through cornfields before a dip down and up through the valley of Fulfen Slade takes us up past Debden radar station with its tall scanner mast, and ahead of us we shall soon see the prominent redbrick water tower of Saffron Walden. Passing it we drop straight down into the busy town, turning right as we meet a T-junction to bring us to the top end of the High Street by the war memorial.

Saffron Walden has its origins in prehistoric times and owes its curious name to the autumn crocus or saffron, widely cultivated hereabouts in the Middle Ages for its yellow dye, much in demand, and also for use in medicine and perfumery. The saffron trade, along with wool and general agricultural produce, brought the town great prosperity, reflected in the many handsome buildings it contains, most noticeably the church, standing high on the north side of the town and dominating the High Street as we drop down it. Although dating from the 13th century, its spire was not added till 1832, making it a rival to Thaxted as one of the finest churches in Essex.

At the foot of the High Street we turn right at the traffic lights on the B184 until we reach the junction where the B1052 forks left. Before this, however, we might like to turn aside on our left to look at the delightful Market Square where the old Corn Exchange now houses the public library. The church peers over from behind and for me it has a faintly Continental atmosphere.

Regaining our route we fork left on the B1052, climbing as far as the first crossroads where stand the ruins of the 12th century castle, built by the Mandevilles, whose name we shall come across again in our last expedition. Beyond it is the town museum. We turn right on Ashdon Road, alongside the Common where there is the largest turf maze in England, at its eastern end. We go on past nondescript houses to the edge of the town and begin a steady climb which will last for several miles through tree-shaded verges. We bear left at a junction in a couple of miles, still climbing, till eventually the country opens out and we are within sight of Ashdon church. It feels like the top of the world up here; we are in the midst of England's corn belt and in summer the rolling hills are a golden blaze of ripening corn, chequered with the dark green of tree-sprinkled hedgerows. Rolling gently down towards Ashdon church much of what we see in the distance ahead is actually Cambridgeshire, we are within a mile of the county boundary. On past the church we descend more steeply through the long and shady village till we come to the Rose and Crown pub and make a sharp right turn. We now have to pay for our coast down into the valley of the little River Bourne with a stiff climb up once more to the open summits where we can undulate pleasantly along to meet the B1054 at the Plough Inn on the outskirts of Radwinter. Turning left brings us in a couple more undulating miles to Hempstead where we bear left with the B1054 into the centre of the sleepy village. Hempstead's chief claim to fame is as the birthplace of the notorious highwayman Dick Turpin in 1705. The Bluebell Inn on our left lays claim to being the actual place of his birth and if we nip inside for some much-needed refreshment we shall find displayed an account of his nefarious career. However, there are other houses nearby which also make the same claim and at this distance of time it is difficult to establish which is the true claimant. Nevertheless, there seems no doubt that the inn, then called the Bell, was in the hands of the Turpin family and may well have the strongest foundation. At some time the name of the inn was changed to the Rose and Crown, but I am informed that owing to poor management in recent years it acquired a bad reputation and the present owners changed it yet again to the Bluebell. Certainly on my brief acquaintance I have no complaints on the current level of service. The sharp-eyed might notice a mis-spelling of Haverhill on the signpost opposite the Bluebell, perhaps attributable to the Essex tendency to drop the letter 'h' in the middle of a word.

Hempstead was the home of the Harvey family, of whom Dr William Harvey discovered the circulation of the blood and lies buried in the churchyard after dying in 1657 at the age of 80. According to Richard Pusey's *Essex Rich and Strange*, the diarist John Aubrey knew him well and was at the funeral.

Climbing yet again out of Hempstead we then have a somewhat easier few miles along the B1054 until we reach Steeple Bumpstead. Here we bear right into Church Street where there is a ford, a mere trickle when I reconnoitred the route in the broiling summer of 1995, but a torrent across the road after a wet winter. At the top end of Church Street stands the medieval Moot Hall, similar in style to that at Thaxted but very much smaller and looking a mite in need of maintenance on my last visit. Steeple Bumpstead is an ancient village, mentioned in the Domesday Book, but the modern manners displayed by a minority visiting the pub behind the Moot Hall suggested that the name could well become corrupted to Steeple Bumptious!

However, let that pass, and on with our ride. Bearing right emerging from Church Street we continue to climb steadily until we level out on to a plateau and, ignoring any minor roads to left or right, have a pleasant, winding couple of miles before us to Cornish Hall End. On the outskirts of the village is a narrow turning on our right signposted The Sampfords. This lane meanders comfortably along past isolated cottages till we reach a dogleg crossroads where we make a right and left, continuing for over a mile until we meet a T-junction. A right turn brings us shortly to the pleasant village of Great Sampford. Passing the Red Lion Inn, or possibly stopping - I recall it as a most welcoming house some years ago - we turn sharp right at the church. After three more miles of considerable undulations we arrive back at the Plough Inn at Radwinter, seen earlier in our ride, and turn left into the village itself. Radwinter is another pleasant place and has sought to preserve its air of peacefulness by introducing carriageway 'pinches' at the edges of the village as a traffic-calming measure - I wish it all success.

Our route lies straight ahead through Radwinter, leaving the church on our left until in half a mile we find a lane on the left signposted to Wimbish. This delightful little road spins us along through a green shade and down across a stream, the headwaters of the River Pant, in actuality our old friend the Blackwater which, for reasons unknown, changes its name above Braintree. After a climb to Tye Green we turn right and in a mile meet the B184 where we turn right again. We are reaching the last miles of our ride now and in a quarter of a mile turn left in obedience to a sign for Newport. Before long we are passing the remnants of the former Debden RAF station, now Carver Barracks, the base for an army regiment of engineers and, on the far side, home to the radar station we passed earlier.

Beyond the old airfield we rejoin our outward route, coasting down past Debden Park before tackling the stiffest climb of the day and the welcome drop down into Newport and the end of our circuit.

The Bluebell Inn, Hempstead; reputedly the birthplace of Dick Turpin

CHAPTER 15

Chipping Ongar - Norton Mandeville - Norwood End - Matching
Green - Moreton - Chipping Ongar.
23 miles. Undulating road work, some bridlepaths.
OS Landranger sheet 167.

In the last ride of our explorations we shall connect the first
two rides in this little series with a recapitulation of what is, for
me at any rate, the essential Essex. It is a fairly short route but
for those of us who like to get well off the beaten track we shall
cover a little of what used to be termed 'rough-stuff' before
mass mountain-bike enthusiasm re-christened it 'off-road' riding.
However, for me it is still rough-stuff, as some of us were doing
this sort of thing before ever mountain-bikes were thought of;
indeed, back in the 1890s at least one enterprising tourist took
a Dursley Pedersen over the Nant Rhyd Willim pass in North
Wales, complete with about 70 pounds of camping and
photographic gear. Those of us who have followed in his
wheelmarks have tended to take our pleasure quietly rather than
in the brash and competitive manner of some modern mountain-
bikers and we shall conduct our present ride in the old way.

Essex, of course, has nothing to offer of the severity of the
Nant Rhyd Willim or Scotland's Lairig Ghru, but at the same
time we shall be well advised to use stoutish wheels and tyres.

This is the only ride in which we shall not be starting from
immediate rail access, although in fact we begin from the
recently defunct Chipping Ongar station. Those travelling by
train will need to ride the six or seven miles from the nearest
available stations at Epping or Brentwood, although there is the
possibility the recently defunct Ongar station will once again
become usable under the auspices of a preservation society,
mentioned in Chapter 1. In the meantime the apparently
convenient car park at that station should not be used; wheel-

clamping has been threatened. If we make the Budworth Hall tea rooms in the High Street our nominal starting point, we shall find two car parks close by. However, both demand payment and height restrictions need watching if we carry machines on roof-racks. The alternative is a free car and lorry park at the bottom end of the town by the river bridge.

The observant will have noticed that I have omitted reference to Bartholomew's map in the chapter heading. This is because the generally excellent Bart's has ever been unreliable in the matter of bridlepaths and in one instance, to be referred to in its place, an entire stretch of public highway is omitted.

On with the ride then southwards down Chipping Ongar High Street. As the name 'Chipping' implies, it is an old market town, still bustling and noisy with traffic and retaining much of its character with elegant buildings on either side as we drop down the hill to cross Cripsey Brook at the bottom. We bear half-left up a sharp climb to Marden Ash where we turn left at the roundabout on to the A128. In a quarter of a mile, opposite the Stag Inn, we turn left as the main road swings right and drop down a long hill with countryside opening out, to Hallsford Bridge where we cross the River Roding. Immediately beyond the bridge we make a sharp left turn and climb steeply up past large gravel workings on the right and then bear left past the local refuse tip, fortunately quite well camouflaged.

After levelling out to an easier gradient for half a mile we shall find a bridlepath on our right beside a cottage. The gate will probably be locked but there is room at the side for cycles and horses and we can ride ahead on a metalled surface with trees to our left and open fields on our right, the view stretching away to the prominent telecommunications mast at Kelvedon Hatch. We climb steadily ahead until we find ourselves entering the farmyard of Paslow Hall. The surface becomes loose and gritty here, demanding some care,and we shall probably find a gate barring our way ahead; but as before, there is a gap at the left to wriggle a cycle through and we continue past some stables on to firm road again with an attractive pond on the right and Paslow Hall itself lying back on the left.

In two hundred yards our bridlepath finishes at King Street where we turn right, climbing gently still, passing the Wheatsheaf Inn, or not, as thirst decrees, to the junction with Rookery Road where we turn left. We have traversed this piece of road in the opposite direction in Chapter 2 and now have to climb gently to Norton Heath to meet the A414. Traffic moves fast here and we must turn right with care for two hundred yards till we meet a road on the left to take us into the village itself. We turn left again opposite the café, which will offer us a good cheap fry-up if we need it, through the woodland to take the first turning on the left past Norton Manor, unsignposted and marked as a dead-end. Once past some plain cottages on the left it becomes an entrancing lane, dipping and winding quietly through hedgerows and open fields for over a mile till we reach the tiny hamlet with the resounding name of Norton Mandeville. Norman it must be in origin and the flint walls of the little church on our left betoken a settlement a good deal older than the fine but strangely contrasting Victorian red-brick of the Hall and its attendant cottages and outbuildings. The church appears to have no electricity supply and the interior is lit by Victorian oil lamps; it also contains a magnificently ornate harmonium.

The metalled road finishes here but there are two bridlepaths ahead of us. Ours is the one straight ahead, usually gated but with the useful gap at the right, which bears away right, around the back of the Hall. The surface is now grassy gravel but easily rideable. Shortly we pass a house on the right and turn sharp right beyond it, following ahead and then bearing left to emerge at the back of one of the dispersal points of the now disused Willingale airfield. I made mention of this World War II American bomber base in Chapter 2 and need not enlarge here except that since writing that chapter I have been told that the film actor James Stewart was supply officer here for a time. So perhaps we can pedal on in reflected glory as we turn out rightwards on to the old perimeter track, now forming part of our bridleway. The concrete surface has suffered grievously from the weather and farm vehicles over the last half century; there is plenty of grit and numerous large pot-holes and a good deal of care is needed. Yet the effort is worth while; there is a peacefulness here and a feeling of great space, a tonic for those maybe too much hemmed in by bricks and mortar in their everyday lives. On the right we shall find a landscaped pond, home for many waterfowl, and few will resist the temptation to lean on the handlebars awhile here.

Beyond the pond we climb a little and then bear sharp left. We pass bumpily through an area evidently used for some kind of motoring activity as there are old car tyres arranged to form a course; the place resembles a rubbish dump in contrast to the surrounding scene. Beyond this we take the next turning right, on to one of the old runways, and then the next left near a large blister hangar. We then go straight forward slightly uphill ignoring a turning on the right; this is one of several private farm roads hereabouts, best avoided as local people have been known to take umbrage at cyclists using them. We shall soon find ourselves on another dispersal point and by following half right to its further side will find our path going onwards past a conifer plantation on the right to meet a public road once more.

We turn left here, on a road again travelled in the opposite direction in Chapter 2, but only until we find a narrow lane going straight ahead at the next junction, signposted to Miller's Green. It winds delightfully downhill and if we divert to the right to the hamlet of Miller's Green itself we shall find what I confidently assert is the longest ford in England, the track running along the bed of a stream for close on half a mile. I did negotiate it one summer day many years ago, finishing up wading with shoes and socks round my neck and the bicycle held over my head; so after a look at this ford among fords we shall retrace to our little lane and continue downhill across the Roding. Here we meet another road from Chapter 2 where we turn left for a mile until we encounter the B184, turning left yet again towards Fyfield.

Just on the outskirts of the village, opposite the Black Bull Inn is a narrow lane signposted, somewhat obscurely, to Norwood End only. This is our route and after a sharp right turn in a short distance we wind along delightfully through gentle country, ignoring a road to Malting Farm, till, just beyond the scattered houses of Norwood End, we take a left fork. In half a mile the road ends but a public byway continues ahead, overhung with trees. The surface is plain mud but although used by farm vehicles is rideable with care in summer although I can't vouch for its condition in the depths of a wet winter. After nearly half a mile going forward we emerge from the trees and swing right. There are some large farm buildings visible to our left and if we aim for these as we bear left at the next junction of tracks we shall find firm road again at Cobbler's Pieces.

A right turn takes us imperceptibly downhill towards Abbess Roding. In spring the roadside verges along here are sprinkled with primroses and dog violets, both species much more common now than in my youth when countryside visitors seemed obsessed with digging up wild flowers by the roots. We swoop down and up through Abbess Roding, little more than a hamlet with a graceful church, and climb to the next junction where our way turns left into a lane running straight and level between hedgerows. In the distance to the right we can see the church and windmill at White Roding, the former having lost its spire and the latter its sails since I first rode this way.

At the next junction we continue ahead gradually bearing to the left until we meet a sharp right-hand bend at Fairlands. On the left is a memorial to US airmen killed in action during World War II while serving at Matching Green airfield, the remains of which are just ahead of us. We shall already have noticed the tall water tower which once served it and we are now passing other dilapidated and overgrown buildings, obviously of military origin. As we pass a sign indicating Anchor Lane Nurseries we are crossing the old perimeter track at a spot which has particular memories for me and many others of my generation. Like Willingale airfield, Matching Green was used for cycle racing in the years following World War II and in 1948 the Olympic trials were held here. The finish area was right at this spot and, together with hundreds of other young clubmen, I spent many happy hours here during that rain-soaked summer, watching our heroes vying for their places in the team. Our road leads on across what was the centre of the airfield. As a result it was completely obliterated by the construction of the airfield and not reinstated until some twenty years after the war, and even now the entire length of road from the junction north of Abbess Roding to Matching Green is omitted from even the latest edition of Bartholomew's maps.

The control tower still exists, in private ownership, and half-way across the open airfield there is an avenue of trees on the right marking the course of one of the runways. On the opposite side it continues as a bridlepath, grass-grown at first, giving way to concrete after a quarter of a mile. Taking this will bring us around the back of a building topped by a radar scanner, purpose unknown, and bumpily down to road at Hull Green, just south of Matching Green village. Turning right brings a junction and a left turn into a road marked 'Unsuitable for Motor Vehicles' yet given priority by the white lining at the junction. One never ceases to wonder at the curious logic of authority!

Despite the warning the lane is well-surfaced although it was not always so, having been let deteriorate since the days when hundreds of cyclists used to hurtle homewards through these lanes, inspired by exploits witnessed on Matching Green airfield. A tributary of Cripsey Brook accompanies us closely from aptly-named Waterman's End and in winter this road is prone to serious flooding. Even a heavy summer storm will put the ford over the road. Not that this deters hardy cyclists; I've seen clubmen riding through in cheerful bravado with water over their bottom brackets.

It is a pleasant road and by riding straight ahead at the next two junctions and bearing left at the third we shall arrive in Moreton, where we might like to take advantage of one or other of the two pubs already noted in Chapter 1.

Crossing the bridge over Cripsey Brook we bear left and uphill for a quarter of a mile before an agreeable last couple of miles along the valley of Cripsey Brook takes us to the last climb up through the houses of Shelley and back into Chipping Ongar.

The U.S.A.F. Memorial at Matching Green

INDEX TO THE PRINCIPAL VILLAGES AND TOWNS

In the Hush

poems by

Susan Woods Morse

Finishing Line Press
Georgetown, Kentucky